COLUMBIA

1000

WORDS YOU

MUST KNOW

for SAT.

BOOK TWO WITH ANSWERS

Richard Lee, Ph.D.

COLUMBIA PRESS

Copyright © 2013 by Richard Lee, Columbia Press

All rights reserved.

No part of this book may be reproduced or distributed in any form or by any means without the written permission of the copyright owner.

All inquiries should be addressed to:

Columbia Press International

803-470 Granville Street

Vancouver, BC V6C 1V5

Email: richardleephd@hotmail.com

ISBN-13： 978-1-927647-24-0

To Nancy, Philip, and Christina

CONTENTS

TO THE STUDENT..ix

Unit 1..12
    jocund, refund, rotund, moribund, rubicund
    laborious, pernicious, avaricious, inauspicious, prejudicious

Unit 2..16
    lacerate, advocate, consolidate, intimidate, precipitate
    lambent, nascent, imminent, penitent, pertinent

Unit 3..20
    lampoon, lagoon, monsoon, platoon, tycoon
    largess, digress, duress, obsess, transgress

Unit 4..24
    legion, fusion, precision, profusion, introversion
    lucrative, abortive, conducive, cumulative, diminutive

Unit 5..28
    lull, dull, gull, null, skull
    lurid, rid, acrid, forbid, rigid

Unit 6..32
    malediction, friction, addiction, conviction, jurisdiction
    malign, align, assign, consign, resign

Unit 7..36
    materiality, brutality, fatality, formality, morality
    mercenary, adversary, centenary, mortuary, planetary

Unit 8..40
    mitigate, innate, emulate, oscillate, propagate
    mollify, certify, ossify, vilify, rectify

Unit 9..44
    mordant, penchant, petulant, rampant, recalcitrant
    morose, compose, dispose, foreclose, verbose

Unit 10..48
    mundane, humane, insane, profane, hurricane
    munificent, consent, extent, aliment, regiment

Unit 11..52
    nefarious, precarious, vicarious, multifarious, temerarious
    nemesis, thesis, mimesis, exegesis, telekinesis

Unit 12..56
    neophyte, byte, acolyte, proselyte, troglodyte
    neoteric, generic, numeric, atmospheric, esoteric

Unit 13..60
    nettle, fettle, mettle, settle, unsettle
    niggard, bard, discard, retard, safeguard

Unit 14..64
    noxious, precious, nutritious, obnoxious, ostentatious
    nugatory, mandatory, purgatory, signatory, defamatory

Unit 15..68
    obeisance, askance, enhance, nuance, renaissance
    obfuscate, castigate, deprecate, articulate, inveterate

Unit 16..72
    objurgate, enunciate, exculpate, extrapolate, facilitate
    obtrude, delude, aptitude, lassitude, rectitude

Unit 17..76
    odious, factious, facetious, fortuitous, disputatious
    oligarchy, anarchy, monarchy, hierarchy, patriarchy

Unit 18..80
    opalescent, ferment, fervent, putrescent, adolescent
    opprobrious, captious, horrendous, lecherous, mellifluous

Unit 19..84
    originate, inculcate, instigate, litigate, immaculate
    ozone, clone, condone, cyclone, silicone

Unit 20..88
    palpable, viable, tractable, immutable, irreparable
    paradox, jukebox, smallpox, equinox, orthodox

Unit 21..92
    parity, brevity, alacrity, depravity, disparity
    parsimonious, arduous, amorphous, ambiguous, anonymous

Unit 22..96
    paucity, probity, frugality, humility, impunity
    penury, fury, jury, , mercury, perjury

Unit 23...100
    perdition, aspersion, abnegation, adulation, implication
    peremptory, allegory, dilatory, inventory, perfunctory

Unit 24...104
    perfidious, tenuous, momentous, ominous, vociferous
    peruse, fuse, muse, abuse, interfuse

Unit25..108
    pervasive, abrasive, dissuasive, evasive, persuasive
    petition, rendition, acquisition, coalition, intuition

Unit 26...112
    polemic, endemic, systemic, epidemic, epistemic
    portend, blend, amend, apprehend, reprehend

Unit 27...116
    precept, concept, incept, inept, intercept
    precocious, spacious, specious, atrocious, ferocious

Unit 28...120
    preponderate, prate, profligate, elaborate, repudiate
    prerogative, correlative, derivative, figurative, preservative

Unit 29...124
    prognosis, hypnosis, diagnosis, scoliosis, tuberculosis
    prolific, horrific, specific, terrific, colorific

Unit 30...128
    prognosticate, implicate, reiterate, relegate, eradicate
    propitiate, deviate, initiate, mediate, differentiate

Unit 31...132
    protocol, menthol, alcohol, parasol, cholesterol
    provident, diffident, evident, incident, coincident

Unit 32...136
    puerile, agile, docile, exile, futile
    purloin, adjoin, conjoin, disjoin, rejoin

Unit 33...140
    purview, preview, review, worldview, interview
    putrefy, classify, justify, qualify, sanctify

Unit 34...144

quagmire, acquire, aspire, conspire, respire
quarantine, chlorine, cuisine, marine, pristine

Unit 35..148
quintessence, sequence, diligence, indulgence, intelligence
quizzical, radical, illogical, sabbatical, chronological

Answer Key..152

Word Index..161

Acknowledgments..175

About the Author..177

TO THE STUDENT

> The shortest and best way of learning a language is to know the roots of it, that is, those original primitive words from which other words are formed.
>
> -- Lord Chesterfield

Columbia 1000 Words You Must Know for SAT presents 1000 most frequently tested words for SAT. You will find 100 vocabulary-building lessons in Books 1 – 3. Each lesson contains 10 new words and they are first presented to you with **Memory Tips**; next, **New Words** are listed in rhyming memory groups and followed by **Sample Sentences**; the last part of the lesson are **Sentence Completion** and **Definition Matching** practice tests with answers. One of the most outstanding features of this book is that each new word is repeated at least five times in a lesson so that you will have a much better chance to memorize it more easily.

Columbia 1000 Words You Must Know for SAT is designed to help you master all the absolutely essential SAT words using our most effective memory method: **A Roots and Rhyming Memory Approach**. Let's take the word "**aberration**" for example and see how this exciting new memory method can help you find the shortest and best way to memorize new words and build a large vocabulary:

1. MEMORY TIPS: Memorizing words with the help of Roots, Prefixes, and Suffixes.

   ion   condition or action; as ***aberration***, *ration, inflation, temptation, abbreviation*

2. NEW WORDS: New Words are arranged in rhyming groups for easy memory.

aberration	*ration*	*inflation*	*temptation*	*abbreviation*

ABERRATION [ˌæbəˈreɪʃ(ə)n] *n.* departure from what is right or true   **rhyming sound –ation**

3. **SAMPLE SENTENCES**: Sample Sentences are given to help you memorize words in context.

   *This complexity is not an **aberration** or something to be wished away, it is the new reality.*

4. **SENTENCE COMPLETION**: Sentence Completion is designed to help you memorize words through tests.

   *The patient's only _____ was a temporary lapse of memory. (**aberration**)*

5. **DEFINITION MATCHING**: Definition Matching is designed to help you memorize words through repetition.

   *departure from what is right or true _____ (**aberration**)*

In this example, the repeated appearance of the word "**aberration**" in the lesson makes it easy for you to memorize. Therefore you can see that only by repeated practice or reinforcement of a new word under different circumstances can you really memorize it so unconsciously that you will never forget. Human memory, like the unconscious, is structured like a language. Once you have memorized a new word, it will stay in your unconscious and become part of yourself. Whenever you need it, it will come to you automatically just like the flowers coming in the spring: it is natural!

Columbia 1000 Words You Must Know for SAT is both a self-help book and a textbook for classroom use. It is the only vocabulary book you will ever need to master the most often tested words on the SAT. If you can spend about 25 minutes a day with this book, you will definitely help yourself expand your vocabulary, build up your word power, and raise your score on the SAT.

Richard Lee, Ph.D.

Beautiful Vancouver

UNIT 1

MEMORY TIPS:

Word building with Roots, Prefixes, and Suffixes:

in	not; as *inauspicious*
ious	characterized by; as *laborious, pernicious, avaricious, inauspicious*
pre	before; as *prejudicious*
re	back, again; as *refund*

NEW WORDS

jocund	refund	rotund	moribund	rubicund
laborious	pernicious	avaricious	inauspicious	prejudicious

1. JOCUND ['dʒɑkənd] *adj.* happy and cheerful   **rhyming sound –und**

   Mary could not but be gay in such a **jocund** company on campus.

   Word Families: **jocundity** *n.*; **jocundly** *adv.*

2. refund ['ri,fʌnd] *v.* to pay back; *n.* return of money

   We offer guaranteed **refund** of any defective goods in our store.

   Word Families: **refundable** *adj.*

3. rotund [roʊ'tʌnd] *adj.* round and fat; having a full and rich sound

He was a large **rotund** man with a very jovial nature and a compassionate disposition.

4. **moribund** ['mɔrə,bʌnd] *adj.* no longer effective and not likely to continue for much longer

The US dollar is **moribund** just like the nation it represents today.

Word Families: **moribundity** *n*

5. **rubicund** ['rubɪkənd] *adj.* having a red face

The woman's **rubicund** face expressed consternation and fatigue.

6. **LABORIOUS** [lə'bɔriəs] *adj.* involving great prolonged effort   **rhyming sound -ious**

The process was **laborious**, but I had no reason to complain of the way it miraculously worked.

7. **pernicious** [pər'nɪʃəs] *adj.* very dangerous or harmful, especially to one's character

We did what we could, but her mother's influence on her was **pernicious**.

Word Families: **perniciousness** *n.;* **perniciously** *adv.*

8. **avaricious** [,ævə'rɪʃəs] *adj.* showing an unreasonable desire to obtain and keep money

The man is so **avaricious** that we call him a blood sucker.

Word Families: **avariciousness** *n.;* **avarice** *n.;* **avariciously** *adv.*

9. **inauspicious** [,ɪnɔ'spɪʃəs] *adj.* unlucky, likely to have an unfavorable outcome

For the Americans, number 13 is considered as an **inauspicious** number.

Word Families: **inauspiciousness** *n.;* **inauspiciously** *adv.*

10. **prejudicious** [,prɛdʒə'dɪʃəs] *adj.* damaging to career and reputation

The reporter's coverage was **prejudicious** to the mayor's campaign.

SENTENCE COMPLETION

Choose one of the new words to complete each sentence below. Make changes if necessary.

jocund	refund	rotund	moribund	rubicund
laborious	pernicious	avaricious	inauspicious	prejudicious

1. People tend to believe that it is _inauspicious_ to walk under a ladder.
2. Our boss is a pleasant _rotund_ little man; he always looks very well-fed.
3. We should not despise plain features, nor a _laborious_ yet honest occupation.
4. I could not but be gay in such a _jocund_ company.
5. The little girl watched the color drain from her father's _rubicund_ face.
6. Smoking is absolutely _pernicious_ to our health.
7. The US dollar, a once proud and honest currency, is _moribund_, like the nation it represents.
8. Almost all stores will _refund_ your money if you're not happy with your purchase.
9. The _prejudicious_ report about the Governor's affairs contributed to his downfall.
10. This businessman is so _avaricious_ that everybody calls him a blood sucker.

DEFINITION MATCHING

Choose one of the new words to match each definition below

jocund	refund	rotund	moribund	rubicund
laborious	pernicious	avaricious	inauspicious	prejudicious

11. round and fat — _rotund_
12. involving great prolonged effort — _laborious_
13. having a red face — _rubicund_
14. damaging to career and reputation — ~~avaricious~~ _prejudicious_
15. to pay back — _refund_

16. very dangerous or harmful   pernicious
17. unreasonably desiring to obtain and keep money   avaricious
18. no longer effective and not likely to continue   moribund
19. unlucky   inauspicious
20. happy and gay   jocund

WRITING SENTENCES

Use each new word in the box to write an original sentence.

| jocund | refund | rotund | moribund | rubicund |
| laborious | pernicious | avaricious | inauspicious | prejudicious |

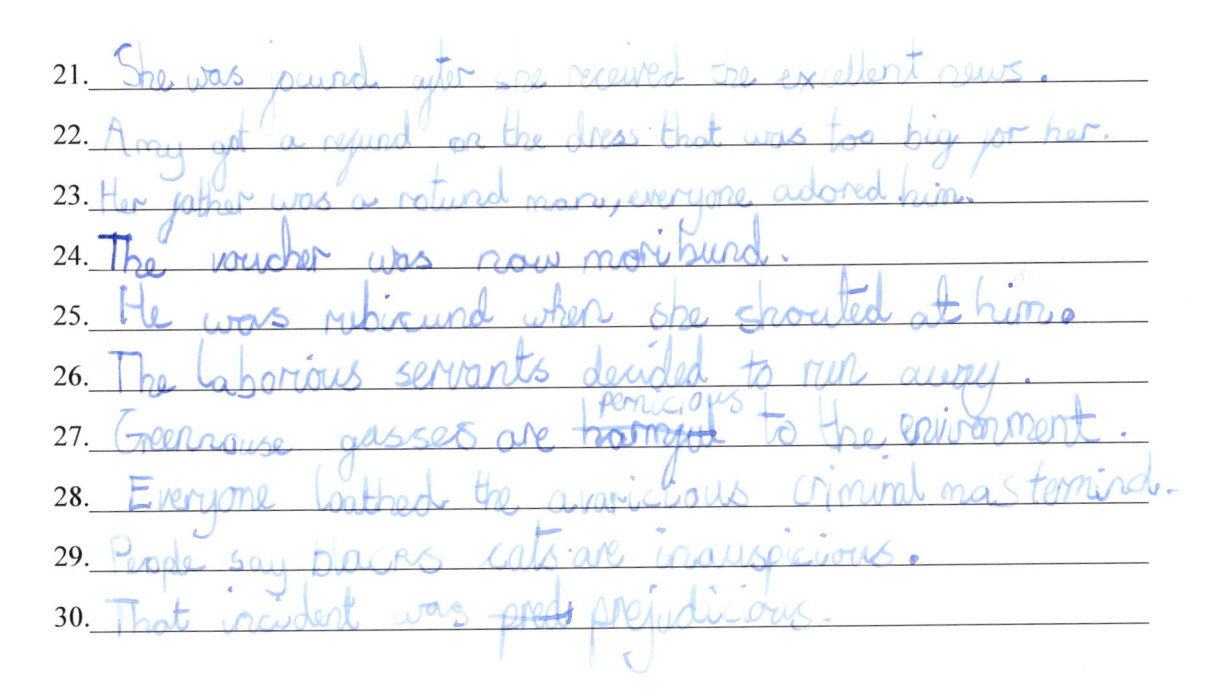

21. She was jocund after she received the excellent news.
22. Amy got a refund on the dress that was too big for her.
23. Her father was a rotund man, everyone adored him.
24. The voucher was now moribund.
25. He was rubicund when she shouted at him.
26. The laborious servants decided to run away.
27. Greenhouse gasses are pernicious to the environment.
28. Everyone loathed the avaricious criminal mastermind.
29. People say black cats are inauspicious.
30. That incident was prejudicious.

UNIT 2

MEMORY TIPS:

Word building with Roots, Prefixes, and Suffixes:

ate	one who; as *lacerate, advocate, consolidate, intimidate, precipitate*
im, in	into, in, on; as *imminent, intimidate*
nasc	be from, to spring forth; as *nascent*
pre	before; as *precipitate*

NEW WORDS

lacerate	advocate	consolidate	intimidate	precipitate
lambent	nascent	imminent	penitent	pertinent

1. **LACERATE** ['læsə,reɪt] *v.* to make a deep cut in someone's flesh   **rhyming sound –ate**

    The man kept drifting about to find Judy and **lacerate** her with the performance.

    Word Families: **laceration** *n.*

2. **advocate** ['ædvəkət] *v.* to publicly support a policy or a way of doing things; *n.* a lawyer; someone who publicly supports someone or something

    Michael Freeman is a strong **advocate** of prison freedom.

    Word Families: **advocation** *n.*

3. **consolidate** [kən'sɑlɪˌdeɪt] *v.* to make or become stronger or more stable

With the release of his new movie he has **consolidated** his **position** as the country's leading director.
Word Families: **consolidation** *n.*; **consolidator** *n.*

4. **intimidate** [ɪn'tɪmɪˌdeɪt] *v.* to deliberately make someone feel frightened

His vicious attempts to **intimidate** people into voting for the governing party did not work.

Word Families: **intimidation** *n.*; **intimidator** *n.*; **intimidating** *adj.*

5. **precipitate** [prɪ'sɪpɪˌtet] *v.* to cause to happen suddenly; *adj.* done rashly or hastily

Most of our financial problems have been caused by **precipitate** policy making in the past.

Word Families: **precipitable** *adj.*

6. **LAMBENT** ['læmbənt] *adj.* softly gleaming or glowing   **rhyming sound -ent**

There was a continual play of **lambent** fire about her charming eyes.

Word Families: **lambency** *n.*; **lambently** *adv.*

7. **nascent** ['næs(ə)nt] *adj.* beginning or formed recently

The fund management industry in the country is still at a **nascent** stage.

8. **imminent** ['ɪmɪnənt] *adj.* likely or certain to happen very soon

The black clouds show that the storm is **imminent**.

Word Families: **imminence** *n.*; **imminently** *adv.*

9. **penitent** ['penɪtənt] *adj.* feeling sorry for having done wrong

He has grown neither humble nor **penitent** by what has passed.

Word Families: **penitence** *n.*; **penitently** *adv.*

10. **pertinent** ['pɜrt(ə)nənt] *adj.* relevant to something

We shall now consider **pertinent** information on recent developments in cardiac electrophysiology.

Word Families: **pertinence** *n.*; **pertinently** *adv.*

SENTENCE COMPLETION

Choose one of the new words to complete each sentence below. Make changes if necessary.

lacerate	advocate	consolidate	intimidate	precipitate
lambent	nascent	imminent	penitent	pertinent

1. Johnson is a conservative who _advocate_ less government control on business.
2. The _lambent_ glow of fireflies made us feel like we were in a wonderland.
3. She was suffering from a badly _lacerate_ hand.
4. It looks like the country is in _imminent_ danger of war.
5. We should never make _precipitate_ decision in business.
6. China is a _nascent_ economic superpower.
7. The Senate and House hearing rooms are designed to _intimidate_ the witness.
8. She has asked some _pertinent_ questions about the project.
9. Michael Jones _consolidated_ his lead in the National League when he won the latest round.
10. The _penitent_ girl turned her back on the unhappy past and began a new life.

DEFINITION MATCHING

Choose one of the new words to match each definition below.

lacerate	advocate	consolidate	intimidate	precipitate
lambent	nascent	imminent	penitent	pertinent

11. to cause to happen suddenly   _precipitate_

12. relevant to something — pertinent
13. to make or become stronger or more stable — consolidate
14. feeling sorry for having done wrong — penitent
15. to deliberately make someone feel frightened — intimidate
16. to make a deep cut in someone's flesh — lacerate
17. likely or certain to happen very soon — imminent
18. softly gleaming or glowing — lambent
19. beginning or formed recently — nascent
20. to publicly support a policy or action — advocate

WRITING SENTENCES

Use each new word in the box to write an original sentence.

lacerate	advocate	consolidate	intimidate	precipitate
lambent	nascent	imminent	penitent	pertinent

21. She had a painful lacerate.
22. James is a doctor who advocate more medicine.
23. The table was consolidated.
24. The bully intimidated everyone.
25. The clouds It started raining, it was a precipitate.
26. The key was lambent.
27. The hall had nascently been made.
28. A storm was imminent.
29. The kidnapper felt penitent after he got sent to jail.
30. That fact was not pertinent to the subject.

UNIT 3

MEMORY TIPS:

Word building with Roots, Prefixes, and Suffixes:

di	apart, not; as *digress*
ob	against; as *obsess*
trans	across, beyond, change; as *transgress*

NEW WORDS

lampoon	lagoon	monsoon	platoon	tycoon
largess	digress	duress	obsess	transgress

1. LAMPOON [læm'pun] *v.* to satirize or ridicule; *n.* humorous satire ridiculing someone
rhyming sound –oon

He denied praising the North Korean government and said that his intention was to **lampoon** the North Korean regime.

Word Families: **lampooner** *n.;* **lampoonist** *n.*

2. lagoon [lə'gun] *n.* a shallow lake or channel

The **lagoon** was pullulated with dead fish.

3. monsoon [mɑn'sun] *n.* seasonal wind of SE Asia; rainy season accompanying seasonal wind

The south-west **monsoon** sets in during April.

Word Families: **monsoonal** *adj.*

4. platoon [plə'tun] *n.* a small group of soldiers that a lieutenant is in charge of

    Our **platoon** was probing the enemy from an advanced position.

5. tycoon [taɪ'kuːn] *n.* a rich and powerful person

    Russian **tycoon** Boris Berezovsky loses his court battle against Roman Abramovich.

6. LARGESS [lɑr'ʒɛs] *n.* a generous giving, especially of money   **rhyming sound -ess**

    In 2006, the donation had a value of $30 billion, making it the biggest philanthropic **largess** in history.

7. digress [daɪ'grɛs] *v.* to depart from the main subject in speech and writing

    She **digressed** from her prepared speech to pay tribute to the President.

    Word Families: **digression** *n.;* **digressive** *adj.;* **digressively** *adv.*

8. duress [dʊ'rɛs] *n.* compulsion by use of force or threats

    She acknowledged that she had signed the agreement under **duress**.

9. obsess [əb'sɛs] *v.* to worry about something all the time

    A string of scandals is absolutely **obsessing** the United States of America.

    Word Families: **obsession** *n;* **obsessive** *adj.;* **obsessively** *adv.*

10. transgress [trænz'grɛs] *v.* to break (a moral law, custom or religion)

    No one is permitted to have privileges to **transgress** the law.

    Word Families: **transgression** *n.;* **transgressor** *n.*

SENTENCE COMPLETION

Choose one of the new words to complete each sentence below. Make changes if necessary.

lampoon	lagoon	monsoon	platoon	tycoon
largess	digress	duress	obsess	transgress

1. You should be generous and give _largess_ to everyone when you are rich.
2. His inexperience made him easy to _lampoon_.
3. We shall not _digress_ into the history of mechanics.
4. Those who acted under _duress_ shall go unpunished.
5. The _monsoon_ will run to the end of next month.
6. A girdle of islands enclosed the _lagoon_.
7. Equity investors should not _obsess_ over economic growth.
8. His _platoon_ made its way to the pre-arranged rendezvous in the desert.
9. A leading philanthropist and cosmetics _tycoon_ plans to donate 78 Cubist works to the New York Metropolitan Museum of Art.
10. We should not _transgress_ the commandment of the Lord.

DEFINITION MATCHING

Choose one of the new words to match each definition below.

lampoon	lagoon	monsoon	platoon	tycoon
largess	digress	duress	obsess	transgress

11. to depart from the main subject — _digress_
12. to worry about something all the time — _obsess_
13. compulsion by use of force or threats — _duress_
14. rainy season accompanying seasonal wind — _monsoon_
15. to break (a moral law) — _transgress_

16. a rich and powerful person — tycoon
17. a generous giving, especially of money — largess
18. a shallow lake or channel — lagoon
19. a group of soldiers with a lieutenant in charge — platoon
20. to satirize or ridicule — lampoon

WRITING SENTENCES

Use each new word in the box to write an original sentence.

lampoon	lagoon	monsoon	platoon	tycoon
largess	digress	duress	obsess	transgress

21. The mean girl tried to lampoon her.
22. The treasure was in front of the deep lagoon.
23. All the crops were watered during monsoon.
24. The platoon marched into war.
25. My uncle is a kind tycoon.
26. Cameron was a largess.
27. Don't digress the topic.
28. It is not good to be giving a duress.
29. Angela, don't obsess reading that book.
30. The criminal transgresses very often.

UNIT 4

MEMORY TIPS:

Word building with Roots, Prefixes, and Suffixes:

con	together; as *conductive*
di	apart, not; as *diminutive*
ion	act of; as *legion, fusion, precision, profusion, introversion*
ive	relating to; as *lucrative, abortive, conductive, cumulative, diminutive*

NEW WORDS

legion	fusion	precision	profusion	introversion
lucrative	abortive	conducive	cumulative	diminutive

1. **LEGION** ['lidʒən] *n.* a large group or number of people   **rhyming sound –ion**

    Each **legion** contained between 3000 to 6000 soldiers.

2. **fusion** ['fjuʒ(ə)n] *n.* melting; product of fusing; popular music blending styles

    The **fusion** of copper and zinc makes the metal brass.

    Word Families: **fusional** *adj.*

3. **precision** [prɪ'sɪʒ(ə)n] *n.* the quality of being accurate and exact; *adj.* accurate

    Scientific instruments have to be made with great **precision**.

Word Families: **precisionism** *n.;* **precisionist** *n.*

4. profusion [prəˈfjuʒ(ə)n] *n.* a large quantity of something

Everything was there in such **profusion** that we did not know what to take.

5. introversion [ˌɪntrəˈvɜ˞ʒən] *n.* the condition of being folded inward; concern with one's own thoughts and feelings

Of course, America went through a similar period of **introversion** after the Vietnam war.

6. LUCRATIVE [ˈlukrətɪv] *adj.* bringing a lot of money   **rhyming sound -ive**

Michael has found a **lucrative** job in a private equity firm in New York.

Word Families: **lucrativeness** *n.;* **lucratively** *adv.*

7. abortive [əˈbɔrtɪv] *adj.* not finished therefore not successful

They had to abandon their **abortive** attempts to make airplanes.

Word Families: **abortively** *adv.*

8. conducive [kənˈdusɪv] *adj.* creating a situation that helps something to happen

Sometimes the home environment just isn't **conducive** to reading.

9. cumulative [ˈkjumjələtɪv] *adj.* increasing steadily

The process of improvement is a **cumulative** one

Word Families: **cumulativeness** *n.;* **cumulatively** *adv.*

10. diminutive [dɪˈmɪnjətɪv] *adj.* very short or small

The pretty woman was a **diminutive** figure beside her tall husband.

Word Families: **diminutiveness** *n.;* **diminutively** *adv.*

SENTENCE COMPLETION

Choose one of the new words to complete each sentence below. Make changes if necessary.

legion	fusion	precision	profusion	introversion
lucrative	abortive	conducive	cumulative	diminutive

1. In Spring, flowers are blooming in __profusion__ in my front garden.
2. __Precision__ instruments are used to help pilots in guiding their aircraft.
3. High energy environment are not __conducive__ to the retention of organic matter in muds.
4. Her delightful sense of humor won her a ~~profusion~~ __legion__ of friends on campus.
5. It would be an __cumulative__ effort to try to curb inflation this way.
6. His administration was plagued by one petty scandal after another, __abortive__ very damaging.
7. The contrast between extroversion and __introversion__ is entirely superficial.
8. The actress has decided to turn her hobby into a __lucrative__ business.
9. His previous __fusion__ of jazz, pop and African melodies have proved highly successful.
10. We noticed a __diminutive__ figure standing at the entrance.

DEFINITION MATCHING

Choose one of the new words to match each definition below.

legion	fusion	precision	profusion	introversion
lucrative	abortive	conducive	cumulative	diminutive

11. not finished therefore not successful   __abortive__
12. bringing a lot of money   __lucrative__
13. melting; product of fusing   __fusion__
14. very short or small   __diminutive__

15. very exact and accurate — precision
16. increasing steadily — cumulative
17. the condition of being folded inward — introversion
18. a large group or number of people — legion
19. a situation that helps something to happen — conducive
20. large quantity of something — profusion

WRITING SENTENCES

Use each new word in the box to write an original sentence.

legion	fusion	precision	profusion	introversion
lucrative	abortive	conducive	cumulative	diminutive

21. She usually played with a legion.
22. There was a great fusion.
23. Everytime I did it to the precision.
24. There was a profusion of oil.
25. The opposite of extroversion is introversion.
26. Amy's art business was lucrative.
27. The art project was abortive.
28. Her victory happened because of the conducive art.
29. Her marks were cumulative.
30. A diminutive of pegs were in the cloakroom.

UNIT 5

MEMORY TIPS:

Word building with Roots, Prefixes, and Suffixes:

ac	to; as *acrid*
for	before; as *forbid*
id	of, like; as *lurid, acrid, forbid, rigid*

NEW WORDS

lull	dull	gull	null	skull
lurid	rid	acrid	forbid	rigid

1. **LULL**   [lʌl] *n.* a quiet period during a very active or violent situation; *v.* to make someone relaxed enough to sleep   **rhyming sound –ull**

    There was a **lull** in political violence after the election of the current president.

2. **dull**   [dʌl] *adj.* boring or not interesting; *v.* to make a feeling weaker

    Life in a remote mountain village could be very **dull** sometimes.

    Word Families: **dullness** *n;* **dullish** *adj.;* **dully** *adv.*

3. **gull**   [gʌl] *n..* a large black and white bird; someone who is easily tricked; *v.* to cheat or trick someone

    The ivory **gull** often follows polar bears to feed on the remains of seal kills.

4. null   [nʌl] *adj.* with on value or effect; *n.* a zero; *v.* to cancel out or remove

A spokeswoman said the agreement had been declared **null** and void.

5. skull   [skʌl] *n.* the bones of the head; a person's head or his mind

The poor girl was rushed to the hospital and treated for a fractured **skull.**

6. LURID   ['lʊrɪd] *adj.* vivid in shocking detail, sensational; glaring in color   **rhyming sound -id**

The pretty girl always paints her toe nails a **lurid** red or orange.

Word Families: **luridness** *n.*; **luridly** *adv.*

7. rid   [rɪd] *v.* to clear or relieve (of)

It is not always easy to **rid** oneself of the bad habits.

8. acrid   ['ækrɪd] *adj.* pungent, bitter

There seems to be an **acrid** tone to your remarks.

Word Families: **acridity** *n.;* **acridly** *adv.*

9. forbid   [fə'bɪd] *v.* to tell somebody not to do or have something

Brazil's constitution **forbids** the military use of nuclear energy.

10. rigid   ['rɪdʒɪd] *adj.* not easily changed

Her **rigid** adherence to the rules made her very unpopular in the office.

Word Families: **rigidity** *n.;* **rigidness** *n.;* **rigidify** *v.;* **rigidly** *adv.*

SENTENCE COMPLETION

Choose one of the new words to complete each sentence below. Make changes if necessary.

lull	dull	gull	null	skull
lurid	rid	acrid	forbid	rigid

1. The actress will have to get __rid__ of the excess weight on her hips.
2. There was never a __dull__ moment when Jenny was with us.
3. The woman looked at the men in the bar with a smile both __acrid__ and desolate.
4. The minister's revelations of financial corruption were __lurid__ and highly exaggerated.
5. This is just the __lull__ before the storm.
6. It was useless to __forbid__ children to play in the park.
7. You are not supposed to __gull__ your friends and relatives.
8. The old man fell out of his window and cracked his __skull__.
9. If no value can be read from the fact table for a member, the value for that member is set to __null__.
10. The entrance examination was so __rigid__ that half of the students were ruled out.

DEFINITION MATCHING

Choose one of the new words to match each definition below.

lull	dull	gull	null	skull
lurid	rid	acrid	forbid	rigid

11. vivid in shocking detail, sensational — __lurid__
12. to cancel out or remove (a force or effect) — __rid__
13. pungent, bitter — __acrid__
14. to tell somebody not to do something — __forbid__
15. not easily changed — __rigid__
16. a quiet period during a violent situation — __lull__
17. a person's head or his mind — __skull__
18. to cheat or trick someone — __gull__

19. to clear or relieve (of) _____ null _____
20. boring or not interesting _____ dull _____

WRITING SENTENCES

Use each new word in the box to write an original sentence.

lull	dull	gull	null	skull
lurid	rid	acrid	forbid	rigid

21. People go to the gym to get rid of excess weight and stay fit.
22. The gull flew over the beach.
23. The lemon has a very acrid taste.
24. My geography lessons can be very dull.
25. The poor little boy cracked his skull and was taken to the hospital.
26.
27.
28.
29.
30.

UNIT 6

MEMORY TIPS:

Word building with Roots, Prefixes, and Suffixes:

con	together, fully; as *consign, conviction*
ion	condition or action; as *malediction, friction, addiction, conviction, jurisdiction*
mal	bad; as *malediction, malign*
re	back, again; as *resign*

NEW WORDS

malediction	friction	addiction	conviction	jurisdiction
malign	align	assign	consign	resign

1. **MALEDICTION** [ˌmæləˈdɪkʃən] *n.* curse   **rhyming sound –iction**

   It is said that Shakespeare's remains were guarded by a **malediction**.

   Word Families: **maledictive** *adj.*; **maledictory** *adj.*

2. **friction**   [ˈfrɪkʃ(ə)n] *n.* the fact that one thing rubs against another; disagreement

   At any rate, **friction** always manifests itself as a force that opposes motion.

3. **addiction**   [əˈdɪkʃ(ə)n] *n.* a strong need to take illegal or harmful drugs; a strong desire to spend time doing something

The man's **addiction** to drugs propelled him towards a life of crime.

Word Families: **addict** *n.*; **addictive** *adj.*; **addicted** *adj.*

4. conviction [kən'vɪkʃ(ə)n] *n.* firm belief; instance of being convicted

The woman appealed unsuccessfully against her **conviction** for murder.

Word Families: **convict** *n..*; **convict** *v.*

5. jurisdiction [ˌdʒʊrɪs'dɪkʃ(ə)n] *n.* the right or power to make legal decisions; an area where a legal system operates

The British police have no **jurisdiction** over foreign bank accounts.

6. MALIGN [mə'laɪn] *adj.* causing harm; evil in influence or effect; *v.* slander or defame

rhyming sound -ign

In an institutional environment that demanded lying, more **malign** lies could flourish.

Word Families: **malignity** *n.*; **maligner** *n.*; **malignant** *adj.*; **malignly** *adv.*

7. align [ə'laɪn] *v.* to bring (a person or group) into agreement with the policy of another; to play in a line

Conservatives, generally, were sure that Taft would **align** himself with the Old Guard in Congress.

8. assign [ə'saɪn] *v.* to give someone a job to do; to put someone in a particular group

If you wish to **assign** students to the project, follow the instructions above.

Word Families: **assignment** *n.*; **assignor** *n.*; **assigner** *n.*; **assignable** *adj.*

9. consign [kən'saɪn] *v.* to put somewhere; to send (goods)

For decades, many of Malevich's works were **consigned** to the basements of Soviet museums.

Word Families: **consignment** *n*; **consignee** *n.*; **consignor** *n..*

10. resign [rɪ'zaɪn] *v.* to state formally that you are leaving a job permanently

The college president has **resigned** over claims he lied to get the job.

SENTENCE COMPLETION

Choose one of the new words to complete each sentence below. Make changes if necessary.

| malediction | friction | addiction | conviction | jurisdiction |
| malign | align | assign | consign | resign |

1. She underwent aversion therapy for her _____ to smoking.

2. He underscored the fact the ICC has no _____ over Sudan.

3. He was known to the police because of previous _____.

4. The politician was answered with a torrent of _____.

5. If she were to _____, who would take her position?

6. We will _____ the goods to him by express.

7. He likes to _____ innocent people.

8. Oil is put in machinery to reduce the _____.

9. When teachers _____ homework, students usually have an obligation to do it.

10. He has attempted to _____ the Socialists with the environmental movement.

DEFINITION MATCHING

Choose one of the new words to match each definition below.

| malediction | friction | addiction | conviction | jurisdiction |
| malign | align | assign | consign | resign |

11. to place in a line   _____

12. a strong need to take illegal or harmful drugs   _____

13. the power to make legal decisions   _____

14. to put somewhere, to send (goods)   _____

15. the fact that one thing rubs against another   _____

16. instance of being convicted   _____

17. to give up office, a job, etc.; to reconcile   _____

18. causing harm   _____

19. to give someone a job to do   _____

20. curse   _____

WRITING SENTENCES

Use each new word in the box to write an original sentence.

| malediction | friction | addiction | conviction | jurisdiction |
| malign | align | assign | consign | resign |

21. _____

22. _____

23. _____

24. _____

25. _____

26. _____

27. _____

28. _____

29. _____

30. _____

UNIT 7

MEMORY TIPS:

Word building with Roots, Prefixes, and Suffixes:

---

ary	one who, concerning; as *mercenary, adversary, centenary, mortuary, planetary*
cent	hundred; as *centenary*
ity	state or quality; as *materiality, brutality, fatality, formality, morality*

NEW WORDS

materiality	brutality	fatality	formality	morality
mercenary	adversary	centenary	mortuary	planetary

1. **MATERIALITY** [mə,tɪri'ælɪti] *n.* the quality of being physical; consisting of matter
   rhyming sound –ality

   In general, art expresses personal ideas while exploring **materiality** on a human scale.

2. **brutality** [bru'tæləti] *n.* extreme violence, especially when it is deliberately cruel

   The woman accused the police of using unwarranted **brutality**.

   Word Families: **brutal** *adj.*; **brutally** *adv.*

3. **fatality** [fə'tæləti] *n.* a death caused by an accident, war, violence, or disease

Drunk driving **fatalities** have declined dramatically over the past decade.

Word Families: **fatalities** *n. pl.;* **fatal** *adj.;* **fatally** *adv.*

4. **formality** [fɔr'mæləti] *n.* requirement of custom or etiquette; necessary procedure without real importance

This is a **formality** we have to go through

Word Families: **formalities** *n.pl.;* **formal** *adj.;* **formally** *adv.*

5. **morality** [mə'ræləti] *n.* principles of right or wrong behavior

They look like figures representing gluttony in a medieval **morality** play.

Word Families: **moralities** *n.pl..;* **moral** *adj.;* **morally** *adv.*

6. **MERCENARY** ['mɜrs(ə)n,eri] *adj.* influenced by greed; *n.pl.* –aries hired soldiers
rhyming sound -icious

Mercenary men lust only for money and gains.

Word Families: **mercenaries** *n.pl.*

7. **adversary** ['ædvər,seri] *n.* an enemy or opponent

The mayor's political **adversaries** were creating a lot of trouble for him.

Word Families: **adversaries** *n.pl.*

8. **centenary** ['sent(ə)n,eri] *n.* a centennial

The university will celebrate its **centenary** next year!

Word Families: **centenaries** *n.pl.*

9. **mortuary** ['mɔrtʃu,eri] *n.* building where corpses are kept before burial or cremation

A medical institution shall place the corpse of a patient in the **mortuary** in time.

10. **planetary** ['plænə,teri] *adj.* relating to a planet or the planets

The sciences of **planetary** geology have benefited tremendously from these new finds.

SENTENCE COMPLETION

Choose one of the new words to complete each sentence below. Make changes if necessary.

| materiality | brutality | fatality | formality | morality |
| mercenary | adversary | centenary | mortuary | planetary |

1. Law and _____ are the bulwark of society.
2. This regiment was entirely composed of _____ troops
3. It is my conviction, or my delusion, that crime brings its own _____ with it.
4. You can rest assured that nothing has really happened in _____ here.
5. The poll was conducted as part of the Science Museum's events to mark its _____.
6. She didn't like the _____ of the party.
7. New discoveries about Uranus excited _____ astronomers in 1977.
8. The girl was not allowed to see her mother for the last time in the _____.
9. Her personal experience of men was of extreme violence and _____.
10. Both of the wrestlers tried to tumble the _____ with all their strength.

DEFINITION MATCHING

Choose one of the new words to match each definition below.

| materiality | brutality | fatality | formality | morality |
| mercenary | adversary | centenary | mortuary | planetary |

11. building where corpses are kept   _____

12. principles of right or wrong behavior   _____

13. relating to a planet or the planets _____

14. death caused by an accident, war, or disease _____

15. a centennial _____

16. the quality of being physical _____

17. hired soldiers _____

18. an enemy or opponent _____

19. extreme violence when it is deliberately cruel _____

20. requirement of custom or etiquette _____

WRITING SENTENCES

Use each new word in the box to write an original sentence.

materiality	brutality	fatality	formality	morality
mercenary	adversary	centenary	mortuary	planetary

21. _____
22. _____
23. _____
24. _____
25. _____
26. _____
27. _____
28. _____
29. _____
30. _____

UNIT 8

MEMORY TIPS:

Word building with Roots, Prefixes, and Suffixes:

ate	Verb: cause to be; as *mitigate, innate, emulate, oscillate, propagate*
ify	Verb: cause; as *mollify, edify, ossify, vilify, rectify*
in	into, in, on; as *innate*

NEW WORDS

mitigate	innate	emulate	oscillate	propagate
mollify	certify	ossify	vilify	rectify

1. MITIGATE ['miti,geIt] *v.* to reduce the harmful effects of something **rhyming sound –ate**

The doctor has found the ways to **mitigate** her pain.

Word Families: **mitigator** *n.;* **mitigatory** *adj.;* **mitigatable** *adj.*

2. innate ['I,neIt] *adj.* being part of someone's nature; inborn

It seems to me that Americans have an **innate** sense of fairness.

Word Families: **innateness** *n.;* **innately** *adv.*

3. emulate ['emjə,leIt] *v.* to attempt to equal by imitating

It was natural that he should **emulate** his brethren.

Word Families: **emulation** *n.*; **emulator** *n.*; **emulative** *adj.*

4. oscillate ['ɑsɪˌleɪt] *v.* to swing back and forth

Oil markets **oscillated** on the day's reports from Geneva.

Word Families: **oscillation** *n. pl..*; **oscillatory** *adj.*

5. propagate ['prɑpəˌgeɪt] *v.* to spread (information and ideas); to reproduce or breed

They **propagated** political doctrines which promised to drive economic growth.

Word Families: **propagation** *n.*; **propagative** *adj.*

6. MOLLIFY ['mɑləˌfaɪ] *v.* to make someone less angry or upset   **rhyming sound -ify**

The investigation was undertaken primarily to **mollify** pressure groups.

Word Families: **mollification** *n.*; **mollifier** *n.*

7. certify ['sɜrtɪˌfaɪ] *v.* to state officially that something is true or accurate

I **certify** this as a true copy of his letter.

8. ossify ['ɑsɪˌfaɪ] *v.* to cause to become bone; to harden

British society tended to **ossify** and close ranks as the 1930s drew to their close.

Word Families: **ossification** *n.*

9. vilify ['vɪləˌfaɪ] *v.* to attack the character of

He was **vilified**, hounded, and forced into exile by the FBI.

Word Families: **vilification** *n;* **vilifier** *n.*

10. rectify ['rɛktəˌfaɪ] *v.* to correct a problem or mistake

Only an act of Congress could **rectify** the situation

Word Families: **rectification** *n.*; **rectifier** *n.*

SENTENCE COMPLETION

Choose one of the new words to complete each sentence below. Make changes if necessary.

mitigate	innate	emulate	oscillate	propagate
mollify	certify	ossify	vilify	rectify

1. On an oscilloscope, you can see an electrical current _____ up and down.

2. Governments should endeavor to _____ distress.

3. Jennifer tried every means to _____ her angry boss.

4. Missionaries went far afield to _____ their faith.

5. I _____ on my honor that she is innocent.

6. The girl obviously has an _____ talent for music.

7. Measures to increase ventilation will _____ the problem.

8. This disease will make her tendons _____ and her body paralyzed into a statue.

9. Mary did not deserve the _____ she had been subjected to.

10. It is customary for boys to _____ their fathers.

DEFINITION MATCHING

Choose one of the new words to match each definition below.

mitigate	innate	emulate	oscillate	propagate
mollify	certify	ossify	vilify	rectify

11. to attack the character of   _____

12. to correct a problem or mistake   _____

13. to harden _____

14. being part of someone's nature; inborn _____

15. to state officially that something is true _____

16. to swing back and forth _____

17. to attempt to equal by imitating _____

18. to spread (information and ideas) _____

19. to make someone less angry or upset _____

20. to reduce the harmful effects of something _____

WRITING SENTENCES

Use each new word in the box to write an original sentence.

mitigate	innate	emulate	oscillate	propagate
mollify	certify	ossify	vilify	rectify

21. _____
22. _____
23. _____
24. _____
25. _____
26. _____
27. _____
28. _____
29. _____
30. _____

UNIT 9

MEMORY TIPS:

Word building with Roots, Prefixes, and Suffixes:

ant	Adjective: a kind of agent, indication; as *mordant, penchant, petulant, rampant, recalcitrant*
dis	apart, not; as *dispose*
fore	before; as *foreclose*

NEW WORDS

| mordant | penchant | petulant | rampant | recalcitrant |
| morose | compose | dispose | foreclose | verbose |

1. **MORDANT** ['mɔrd(ə)nt] *adj.* sarcastic or scathing; *n.* substance used to fix dyes
   rhyming sound –ant

   The senator's political opponents feared her **mordant** wit.

   Word Families: **mordancy** *n.* ; **mordantly** *adv.*

2. **penchant** ['penʃənt] *n.* a feeling of liking something very much

   American pragmatism produces a **penchant** for examining issues separately.

3. **petulant** ['petʃələnt] *n.* childishly irritable or peevish

The billionaire's daughter is sometimes wayward, **petulant**, and disagreeable.

Word Families: **petulance** *n.;* **petulantly** *adv.*

4. **rampant** ['ræmpənt] *adj.* existing, happening, or spreading in a uncontrolled way

Poverty and disease are **rampant** in rural areas of this country.

Word Families: **rampancy** *n.;* **rampantly** *adv.*

5. **recalcitrant** [rɪ'kælsɪtrənt] *adj.* refusing to obey orders

Besides, even for **recalcitrant** students, there are provisions under the current system to deal with them.

Word Families: **recalcitrance** *n.;* **recalcitrantly** *adv.*

6. **MOROSE** [mə'roʊs] *adj.* feeling unhappy; in a bad mood   **rhyming sound -ose**

The man became at times listless and **morose**.

7. **compose** [kəm'poʊz] *v.* to put together; to form something

The committee is **comprised** of representatives from both the public and private sectors.

8. **dispose** [dɪ'spoʊz] *v.* to place in a certain order; to make somebody willing or receptive to do something

The millionaire was forced to **dispose** of all his treasures.

Word Families: **disposal** *n.;* **disposed** *adj.;* **disposable** *adj.*

9. **foreclose** [fɔr'kloʊz] *v* to take possession of someone's property because he failed to pay back the money borrowed to buy it

The bank **foreclosed** on the mortgage for his previous home.

Word Families: **foreclosure** *n.*

10. **verbose** [vɜr'boʊs] *adj.* using more words than necessary, and therefore long and boring

For the first time, her usually **verbose** husband was willing to listen.

SENTENCE COMPLETION

Choose one of the new words to complete each sentence below. Make changes if necessary.

mordant	penchant	petulant	rampant	recalcitrant
morose	compose	dispose	foreclose	verbose

1. They have an equal and opposite _____ for conspiracy theories.

2. Michael's speech carried a wicked and _____ sense of humor.

3. The girl had grown more than usually _____ and incalculable.

4. She greeted him now as though he were a _____ member of the family, rather than a menacing outsider.

5. His academic writings are usually difficult and _____.

6. Inevitably, many lenders will _____ on the homeowner.

7. These new internet billionaires look just like normal adults, but inside, they are _____, narcissistic children with oversized egos.

8. There was only a small part of his estate that Sir Walter could _____ of.

9. England, Scotland and Wales _____ the island of Great Britain.

10. Malaria is still _____ in some swampy regions.

DEFINITION MATCHING

Choose one of the new words to match each definition below.

mordant	penchant	petulant	rampant	recalcitrant
morose	compose	dispose	foreclose	verbose

11. childishly irritable or peevish   _____

12. using more words than necessary   _____

13. to take possession of someone's property _____

14. refusing to obey orders   _____

15. to make somebody willing to do something _____

16. sarcastic or scathing   _____

17. feeling unhappy, in a bad mood   _____

18. to form something   _____

19. a feeling of liking something very much   _____

20. existing or happening in a uncontrolled way _____

WRITING SENTENCES

Use each new word in the box to write an original sentence.

| mordant | penchant | petulant | rampant | recalcitrant |
| morose | compose | dispose | foreclose | verbose |

21. _____
22. _____
23. _____
24. _____
25. _____
26. _____
27. _____
28. _____
29. _____
30. _____

UNIT 10

MEMORY TIPS:

Word building with Roots, Prefixes, and Suffixes:

con	together; as *consent*
in	not; as *insane*
pro	forward, before; as *profane*

NEW WORDS

mundane	humane	insane	profane	hurricane
munificent	consent	extent	aliment	regiment

1. **MUNDANE** [mʌnˈdeɪn] *adj.* ordinary and not interesting; relating to the world and practical matters   **rhyming sound –ane**

    It was hard to return to **mundane** matters after such a wonderful trip.

    Word Families: **mundanity** *n.;* **mundaneness** *n.;* **mundanely** *adv.*

2. **humane** [hjuˈmeɪn] *adj.* kind or merciful

    Our aim is for a more just and **humane** society.

    Word Families: **humaneness** *n.;* **humanely** *adv.*

3. **insane** [ɪnˈseɪn] *adj.* very stupid or crazy; suffering from severe mental illness

    Joanne would be **insanely** jealous if Bill left her for another woman.

Word Families: **insanely** adj.

4. profane [prə'feɪn] *adj.* showing a lack of respect for God or religion; *v.* to show a lack of respect for God or religion

To smoke in a church or mosque would be a **profane** act.

Word Families: **profanation** n.; **profanity** n.; **profanely** adv.

5. hurricane ['hʌrɪˌkeɪn] *n.* a violent storm with strong wind and heavy rain

During the **hurricane**, many people's homes were destroyed.

Word Families: **hurricanes** n.pl.

6. MUNIFICENT [mju'nɪfɪsənt] *adj.* extremely generous   **rhyming sound -ent**

Dunn is one of the country's most **munificent** artistic benefactors.

Word Families: **munificence** n.; **munificently** adv.

7. consent [kən'sent] *v.* to give approval for something; *n.* permission to do something

To be able to go on a field trip, a written **consent** of the parent is required.

8. extent [ɪk'stent] *n.* range over which something extends, the size or area

The city government itself has little information on the **extent** of industrial pollution in the region.

Word Families: **extents** n.pl.

9. aliment ['æləmənt] *n.* something that feeds or sustains something else

Can we find the mystic **aliment** that would give them vigor?

Word Families: **aliments** n.pl.

10. regiment ['redʒɪmənt] *n.* organized body of troops as a unit of the army

The **regiment** secured its position to attack the enemy.

Word Families: **regimentation** n.; **regimental** adj.

SENTENCE COMPLETION

Choose one of the new words to complete each sentence below. Make changes if necessary.

| mundane | humane | insane | profane | hurricane |
| munificent | consent | extent | aliment | regiment |

1. For an instant, the man became _____, a screaming animal.

2. Nancy is one of the most _____ girls I have ever known.

3. The full _____ of the losses was disclosed yesterday.

4. Everyone has to learn how to do _____ tasks well.

5. The advancement of science and technology is the best _____ to a better society.

6. The _____ blew with such force that trees were uprooted.

7. Mary finally _____ to donate five thousand dollars to the United Way.

8. As he hated the war in Vietnam, Michael decided to desert his _____.

9. These people have _____ the long upheld traditions of the Church.

10. Certainly those who spread the message of God are the most _____.

DEFINITION MATCHING

Choose one of the new words to match each definition below.

| mundane | humane | insane | profane | hurricane |
| munificent | consent | extent | aliment | regiment |

11. organized body of troops as a unit of the army   _____

12. permission to do something   _____

13. something that feeds or sustains something else   _____

14. to show a lack of respect for God or religion   _____

15. the size or area of something   _____

16. ordinary and not interesting _____

17. a violent storm with strong wind and heavy rain _____

18. kind and merciful _____

19. extremely generous _____

20. very stupid or crazy _____

WRITING SENTENCES

Use each new word in the box to write an original sentence.

mundane	humane	insane	profane	hurricane
munificent	consent	extent	aliment	regiment

21. _____

22. _____

23. _____

24. _____

25. _____

26. _____

27. _____

28. _____

29. _____

30. _____

UNIT 11

MEMORY TIPS:

Word building with Roots, Prefixes, and Suffixes:

ious	characterized by; as *nefarious, vicarious, precarious, multifarious, temerarious*
mult	many; as *multifarious*
pre	before; as *precarious*
tele	distance; as *telekinesis*

NEW WORDS

nefarious	precarious	vicarious	multifarious	temerarious
nemesis	**thesis**	**mimesis**	**exegesis**	**telekinesis**

1. **NEFARIOUS** [nɪ'feriəs] *adj.* evil or dishonest   **rhyming sound –arious**

   The man was universally feared because of his many **nefarious** deeds.

   Word Families: **nefariousness** *n.*; **nefariously** *adj.*

2. **precarious** [prɪ'keriəs] *adj.* likely to change or become dangerous without warning

   The company's financial situation has become **precarious**.

   Word Families: **precariousness** *n.*; **precariously** *adv.*

3. **vicarious** [vɪ'keriəs] *adj.* experienced through the actions of other people

Many young people use television as their **vicarious** form of social life.

Word Families: **vicariousness** *n.;* **vicariously** *adv.*

4. **multifarious** [ˌmʌltɪˈferiəs] *adj.* consisting of many different types

Chapter five elaborates territorial states and the **multifarious** cultures.

Word Families: **multifariousness** *n.;* **multifariously** *adv.*

5. **temerarious** [ˌtɛməˈrɛriəs] *adj.* showing a reckless confidence that may be offensive

Some people are just **temerarious** enough to break the rules for their own sake.

Word Families: **temerariously** *adj.*

6. **NEMESIS** [ˈnemǝsɪs] *n.* retribution or vengeance   **rhyming sound -esis**

Some people believe that AIDS is our collective **nemesis**.

Word Families: **nemeses** *n.pl.*

7. **thesis** [ˈθiːsis] *n.* written work submitted for a degree

The fundamental **thesis** of this book goes back to the winter of 1969.

Word Families: **theses** *n.pl.*

8. **mimesis** [mɪˈmisɪs] *n.* acting without the use of words; a rhetorical use of what somebody else might have said

Fictionality and **mimesis** are common in novels.

9. **exegesis** [ˌeksəˈdʒisɪs] *n.* explanation of a text, especially. the Bible

Within this context, Fraser is capable of **exegesis** that goes beyond the obvious.

Word Families: **exegetic** *adj.;* **exegetical** *adj.*

10. **telekinesis** [ˌtelɪkɪˈnisɪs] *n.* the power to move or change objects using your mind

Telekinesis is another ability for which there is little hard evidence.

Word Families: **telekinetic** *adj.*

SENTENCE COMPLETION

Choose one of the new words to complete each sentence below. Make changes if necessary.

nefarious	precarious	vicarious	multifarious	temerarious
nemesis	thesis	mimesis	exegesis	telekinesis

1. A soldier leads a very _____ life.

2. How often we have been _____ and rushed unwisely in.

3. The reasons for closure are _____.

4. The uncanny girl invented fantasy lives for her own _____ pleasure.

5. The playwright uses _____ in his plays.

6. In 1946, General Electric was fined by the American government owing to its _____ wartime activities.

7. Yet the imminent crisis in its balance of payments may be the President's _____.

8. Johnson was awarded his Master of Arts degree for his _____ on Keats.

9. The old man has the ability to manipulate and use magic items via _____.

10. Biblical _____ was a phase of the rational approach to religion that was popular in the Age of Reason.

DEFINITION MATCHING

Choose one of the new words to match each definition below.

nefarious	precarious	vicarious	multifarious	temerarious
nemesis	thesis	mimesis	exegesis	telekinesis

11. the power to move objects using your mind   _____

12. consisting of many different types   _____

13. to become dangerous without warning   _____

14. explanation of a text, especially. the Bible   _____

15. acting without the use of words   _____

16. evil or dishonest   _____

17. written work submitted for a degree   _____

18. showing a confidence that may be offensive   _____

19. retribution or vengeance   _____

20. experienced through the actions of other people   _____

WRITING SENTENCES

Use each new word in the box to write an original sentence.

nefarious	precarious	vicarious	multifarious	temerarious
nemesis	thesis	mimesis	exegesis	telekinesis

21. _____

22. _____

23. _____

24. _____

25. _____

26. _____

27. _____

28. _____

29. _____

30. _____

UNIT 12

MEMORY TIPS:

Word building with Roots, Prefixes, and Suffixes:

ic	of, like; as *neoteric, generic, numeric, atmospheric, esoteric*
neo	new; as *neophyte, neoteric*
pro	forward, before; as *proselyte*

NEW WORDS

neophyte	byte	acolyte	proselyte	troglodyte
neoteric	generic	numeric	atmospheric	esoteric

1. **NEOPHYTE** ['niə,faɪt] *n.* someone who is just learning to do something and doesn't have much experience   **rhyming sound –yte**

    She is just a **neophyte** in politics.

    Word Families: **neophytes** *n.pl.*

2. **byte** [baɪt] *n.* a basic unit for storing computer information, a byte is approximately equivalent to one printed character

    They are intended for character sets where a character does not fit into a single **byte**.

    Word Families: **bytes** *n.pl.*

3. **acolyte** ['ækə,laɪt] *n.* someone who helps an important person

To her **acolytes**, Helen Johnson is just known as "Dragon Lady.".

Word Families: **acolytes** *n. pl.*

4. **proselyte** ['prasə,laɪt] *n.* a new convert to a religious faith or political doctrine

We should allow **proselytes** to enter no matter where they are from.

Word Families: **proselytism** *n.*

5. **troglodyte** ['traglə,daɪt] *n.* cave dweller

He dismissed advocates of a completely free market as economic **troglodytes** with no concern for the social consequences.

Word Families: **troglodytes** *n.pl.*

6. **NEOTERIC** [,niə'tɛrɪk] *adj.* having a contemporary origin   **rhyming sound -eric**

Our products are famous for **neoteric** design and fine craftsmanship.

7. **generic** [dʒə'nɛrɪk] *adj.* of a class, group, or genus

The doctor offered me a choice of a branded or a generic drug.

Word Families: **generics** *n.pl.;* **genrically** *adv.*

8. **numeric** [nu'mɛrɪk] *adj.* numerical

The instructions of the program have to be written in a **numeric** form

Word Families: **numerically** *adv.*

9. **atmospheric** [,ætmə'sfɛrɪk] *adj.* relating to or existing in the atmosphere around the earth or another planet

The barometer marked a continuing fall in **atmospheric** pressure.

Word Families: **atmospherical** *adj.;* **atmospherically** *adv..*

10. **esoteric** [,ɛsə'tɛrɪk] *adj.* known about or understood by very few people

The quantum theory is not just an **esoteric** addendum.

Word Families: **esotericism** *n.;* **esotericist** *n.;* **esoterically** *adv.*

SENTENCE COMPLETION

Choose one of the new words to complete each sentence below. Make changes if necessary.

| neophyte | byte | acolyte | proselyte | troglodyte |
| neoteric | generic | numeric | atmospheric | esoteric |

1. _____ nuclear tests are now banned by an international treaty.

2. The old man is a _____ who doesn't know anything about city life.

3. There are indications that his _____ popularity may be ebbing.

4. They discussed about the possibility of establishing _____ Christian schools in Japan.

5. David was no _____ and had no fancies about the business.

6. A _____ is the smallest unit of processing in any computer architecture.

7. Jenny Houston, an _____ of the U.S. senator, wrote the famous speech on women's rights.

8. The woman is a _____ of the new political party.

9. They encourage doctors to prescribe cheaper _____ drugs instead of more expensive brand names.

10. Do you want to use your _____ keypad instead of the mouse?

DEFINITION MATCHING

Choose one of the new words to match each definition below.

| neophyte | byte | acolyte | proselyte | troglodyte |
| neoteric | generic | numeric | atmospheric | esoteric |

11. the cave dweller   _____

12. known about or understood by very few people _____

13. someone who helps an important person _____

14. having a contemporary origin _____

15. someone who is just learning to do something _____

16. relating to atmosphere around the earth _____

17. numerical _____

18. a basic unit for storing computer information _____

19. of a class, group, or genus _____

20. a new convert to a religion or political doctrine _____

WRITING SENTENCES

Use each new word in the box to write an original sentence.

| neophyte | byte | acolyte | proselyte | troglodyte |
| neoteric | generic | numeric | atmospheric | esoteric |

21. _____
22. _____
23. _____
24. _____
25. _____
26. _____
27. _____
28. _____
29. _____
30. _____

UNIT 13

MEMORY TIPS:

Word building with Roots, Prefixes, and Suffixes:

ard	characterized by; as *niggard, bard, discard, retard, safeguard*
dis	apart, not; as *discard*
re	back, again; as *retard*
un	not; as *unsettle*

NEW WORDS

nettle	fettle	mettle	settle	unsettle
niggard	bard	discard	retard	safeguard

1. NETTLE   ['net(ə)l] *n.* plant with stinging hairs on the leaves; *v.* to annoy someone
rhyming sound –ettle

Michael was **nettled** by her rude manners.

Word Families: **nettled** *adj.*

2. fettle   ['fet(ə)l] *n.* state of health or spirits

She was in fine **fettle** when she returned from her trip to Paris.

3. mettle   ['met(ə)l] *n.* the determination and ability to deal with problems

For both sides, it's the first real test of their **mettle** this season.

Word Families: **mettlesome** *adj.*

4. settle   ['set(ə)l] *n.* a long wooden bench with high back and arms; *v.* to arrange or put in order; to become established as a resident

In an attempt to **settle** the case, Mike has agreed to make full resitution.

Word Families: **settleable** *adj.*

5. unsettle   [ʌn'set(ə)l] *v.* to make someone feel nervous, confused, or upset

The uncertainty is likely to **unsettle** the capital market.

Word Families: **unsettlement n.; unsettlingly** *adv.*

6. NIGGARD   ['nɪgəd] *n.* somebody regarded as stingy or miserly   **rhyming sound -ard**

Never have we seen such a **niggard** like him!

Word Families: **niggardly** *adj.*

7. bard   [bɑrd] *n.* a poet

Byron was her favourite **bard** from the period when she first could feel.

Word Families: **bards** *n.pl.* **bardic** *adj.*

8. discard   [dɪs'kɑrd] *v.* to get rid of something you no longer want

He **discards** his winter underclothing when the weather gets warm.

Word Families: **discardable** *adj.*

9. retard   ['ri,tɑrd] *v.* to delay or slow (process or development)

That unpleasant news might **retard** her recovery

Word Families: retardation n.; **retarded** *adj.*

10. safeguard   ['seɪf,gɑrd] *v.* to protect; *n.* protection

The first duty of a government is to **safeguard** its people against external aggression.

Word Families: **safeguards** *n.pl.*

SENTENCE COMPLETION

Choose one of the new words to complete each sentence below. Make changes if necessary.

| nettle | fettle | mettle | settle | unsettle |
| niggard | bard | discard | retard | safeguard |

1. At first sight, the economy hit the August turmoil in fine _____.

2. Sooner or later, they will have to grasp the _____.

3. We may _____ all apprehensions for the safety of the Union.

4. Nature is prodigal in variety, but _____ in innovation.

5. Continuing violence will _____ negotiations over the country's future.

6. This was one of the first areas to be _____ by Europeans.

7. A system like ours lacks adequate _____ for civil liberties.

8. The girl showed her _____ by winning the contest in spite of her being handicapped.

9. The young _____ wandered all over the country in search of his love.

10. Nothing can _____ his resolution.

DEFINITION MATCHING

Choose one of the new words to match each definition below.

| nettle | fettle | mettle | settle | unsettle |
| niggard | bard | discard | retard | safeguard |

11. to delay or slow   _____

12. to become established as a resident   _____

13. to protect   _____

14. to make someone feel nervous or upset   _____

15. to get rid of something you no longer want   _____

16. to annoy someone   _____

17. a poet   _____

18. a stingy person   _____

19. determination and ability to deal with problems   _____

20. state of health or spirits   _____

WRITING SENTENCES

Use each new word in the box to write an original sentence.

nettle	fettle	mettle	settle	unsettle
niggard	bard	discard	retard	safeguard

21. _____
22. _____
23. _____
24. _____
25. _____
26. _____
27. _____
28. _____
29. _____
30. _____

UNIT 14

MEMORY TIPS:

Word building with Roots, Prefixes, and Suffixes:

de	down, away, from, about; as *defamatory*
ious	characterized by; as *noxious, precious, licentious, obnoxious, ostentatious*
ob	against; as *obnoxious*
ory	a place for; as *purgatory*

NEW WORDS

noxious	precious	nutritious	obnoxious	ostentatious
nugatory	mandatory	purgatory	signatory	defamatory

1. **NOXIOUS** ['nɑkʃəs] *adj.* harmful or poisonous **rhyming sound –ious**

    Heavy industry pollutes our rivers with **noxious** chemicals.

    Word Families: **noxiousness** *n.*; **noxiously** *adv.*

2. **precious** ['prɛʃəs] *adj.* worth of great value and importance; loved and treasured

    Water is becoming an increasingly precious resource.

    Word Families: **preciously** *adj.*

3. **nutritious** [nuˈtrɪʃəs] *adj.* nourishing

    It is always important to choose enjoyable and **nutritious** foods.

Word Families: **nutrition** *n.;* **nutritiously** *adv.*

4. obnoxious [ɑbˈnɑkʃəs] *adj.* very rude. offensive, or unpleasant

It seemed as if the lawyer was deliberately being as **obnoxious** as possible.

Word Families: **obnoxiously** *adv.*

5. ostentatious [ˌɑstɛnˈtɛʃəs] *adj.* showy; pretentiously displaying

Obviously he had plenty of money and was generous in its use without being **ostentatious**.

Word Families: **ostentation** *n.;* **ostentatiously** *adv.*

6. NUGATORY [ˈnugəˌtɔri] *adj.* not important or effective   **rhyming sound -atory**

Her efforts have been totally **nugatory**.

Word Families: **nugatorily** *adv.*

7. mandatory [ˈmændəˌtɔri] *adj.* ordered by a law or rule; *n.* mandatary

The **mandatory** retirement age is 65 in most countries.

Word Families: **mandatories** *n.pl.;* **mandatorily** *adv.*

8. purgatory [ˈpɜrgəˌtɔri] *n.* a place where a penitent souls are purified; an unpleasant place or experience

It is like living in a **purgatory** over here in the big city.

Word Families: **purgatories** *n.pl.;* **purgatorial** *adj.*

9. signatory [ˈsɪgnəˌtɔri] *n.* one of the parties who signs a document

Both parties are **signatories** to the Joint Venture Agreement..

Word Families: **signatories** *n.pl.*

10. defamatory [dɪˈfæməˌtɔri] *adj.* attacking the good reputation of

The company claimed that Google was liable as a publisher of **defamatory** comments.

Word Families: **defamation** *n.*

SENTENCE COMPLETION

Choose one of the new words to complete each sentence below. Make changes if necessary.

| noxious | precious | nutritious | obnoxious | ostentatious |
| nugatory | mandatory | purgatory | signatory | defamatory |

1. Kiwifruit is delicious and _____.

2. Actors, he decided, were too _____ and neurotic.

3. The people at my table were so _____ I simply had to change my seat.

4. _____ gases had built up in the sewer.

5. Any concession made to one _____ country has to be extended to all.

6. For me it was just a transfer from one _____ to another.

7. This is absolutely _____ to worry about the future.

8. That article about the mayor was completely _____.

9. The millionaire's daughter is absolutely not an _____ person anyway.

10. It is _____ for blood banks to test all donated blood for the virus.

DEFINITION MATCHING

Choose one of the new words to match each definition below.

| noxious | precious | nutritious | obnoxious | ostentatious |
| nugatory | mandatory | purgatory | signatory | defamatory |

11. very rude, offensive, or unpleasant   _____

12. an unpleasant place or experience   _____

13. nourishing _____

14. one of the parties who signs a document _____

15. ordered by a law or rule _____

16. harmful or poisonous _____

17. attacking the good reputation of _____

18. showy _____

19. not important or effective _____

20. worth of great value and importance _____

WRITING SENTENCES

Use each new word in the box to write an original sentence.

noxious	precious	nutritious	obnoxious	ostentatious
nugatory	mandatory	purgatory	signatory	defamatory

21. _____

22. _____

23. _____

24. _____

25. _____

26. _____

27. _____

28. _____

29. _____

30. _____

UNIT 15

MEMORY TIPS:

Word building with Roots, Prefixes, and Suffixes:

ance	state of; as *obeisance, askance, enhance, nuance, renaissance*
ate	cause to be; as *obfuscate, castigate, articulate, articulate, inveterate*
in	in, into, on; as *inveterate*
re	back, again; as *renaissance*

NEW WORDS

obeisance	askance	enhance	nuance	renaissance
obfuscate	castigate	deprecate	articulate	inveterate

1. **OBEISANCE** [oʊˈbeɪsəns] *n.* attitude of respect; bow or curtsy   **rhyming sound –ance**

   She made a deep **obeisance** to the Queen.

   Word Families: **obeisances** *n. pl.;* **obeisant** *adj.*

2. **askance** [əˈskæns] *adv.* with doubt or suspicion

   Asian policymakers are entitled to look **askance** at foreign bondholders.

3. **enhance** [ɪnˈhæns] *v..* to improve something or make it more attractive

   Good language skills should **enhance** your chances of getting a job.

   Word Families: **enhancement** *n.;* **enhancer** *n.*

4. nuance ['nu,ɑns] *n.* subtle difference in color, meaning, or tone

With the slightest perceptible **nuance** he opened the way for bribery.

Word Families: **nuances** *n. pl.*

5. renaissance [rɪ'neɪsəns] *n.* revival or rebirth; revival of learning in the 14-16 centuries

Humanism is definitely the essence of **renaissance**.

6. OBFUSCATE ['ɑbfə,skeɪt] *v.* to deliberately make something confusing or difficult to understand   **rhyming sound -ate**

They are **obfuscating** the issue, as only insurance companies can.

Word Families: **obfuscation** *n.;* **obfuscatory** *adj.*

7. castigate ['kæstɪ,geɪt] *v.* to criticize someone or something severely

The woman **castigated** her husband for being stupid and lazy.

Word Families: **castigation** *n.;* **castigator** *n.;* **castigatory** *adj.*

8. deprecate ['deprə,keɪt] *v.* to criticize something strongly

I strongly **deprecate** the use of violence by the students.

Word Families: **deprecation** *n.;* **deprecatory** *adj.;* **deprecatingly** *adv.*

9. articulate [ɑr'tɪkjuleɪt] *adj.* able to express oneself clearly and coherently; *v.* to speak or say clearly and coherently

She was unable to offer an **articulate** description of what had happened.

Word Families: **articulation** *n;* **articulately** *adv.*

10. inveterate [ɪn'vetərət] *adj.* firmly established in a habit or condition

Besides that, not all Americans are **inveterate** huggers anyway.

Word Families: **inveteracy** *n.;* **inveterately** *adv.*

SENTENCE COMPLETION

Choose one of the new words to complete each sentence below. Make changes if necessary.

obeisance	askance	enhance	nuance	renaissance
obfuscate	castigate	deprecate	articulate	inveterate

1. Florence is known as the shrine of _____.

2. He loved the _____ of joy that crossed her face when he touched her.

3. Marx never lost an opportunity to _____ colonialism.

4. When he was rich and powerful, all paid _____ to him.

5. The man failed to _____ what he really wanted to achieve in his startup.

6. Food is there to keep you healthy and _____ your enjoyment of life.

7. Michael was not only an avid reader but also an _____ note-taker.

8. They looked _____ at her and didn't know what to do.

9. Ethiopia rejected the verdict, and has since used diplomatic verbiage to _____ and stall.

10. The fashion now is to _____ the positive contributions of Keynesian economics.

DEFINITION MATCHING

Choose one of the new words to match each definition below.

obeisance	askance	enhance	nuance	renaissance
obfuscate	castigate	deprecate	articulate	inveterate

11. to criticize someone or something severely   _____

12. to criticize something strongly   _____

13. to improve something   _____

14. to speak clearly and coherently   _____

15. firmly established in a habit or condition _____

16. attitude of respect _____

17. to deliberately make something confusing _____

18. subtle difference in color, meaning, or tone _____

19. revival or rebirth _____

20. with doubt or suspicion _____

WRITING SENTENCES

Use each new word in the box to write an original sentence.

obeisance	askance	enhance	nuance	renaissance
obfuscate	castigate	deprecate	articulate	inveterate

21. _____

22. _____

23. _____

24. _____

25. _____

26. _____

27. _____

28. _____

29. _____

30. _____

UNIT 16

MEMORY TIPS:

Word building with Roots, Prefixes, and Suffixes:

apt	fit; as *aptitude*
ate	cause to be; as *objurgate, enunciate, exculpate, extrapolate, facilitate*
ob	against; as *objurgate, obtrude*
tude	state of; as *obtrude, delude, aptitude, lassitude, rectitude*

NEW WORDS

objurgate	enunciate	exculpate	extrapolate	facilitate
obtrude	delude	aptitude	lassitude	rectitude

1. **OBJURGATE** [ˈɑbdʒɚˌget] *v.* to scold somebody angrily   **rhyming sound –ate**

    She **objurgated** him for his insensitive remarks about the homeless people.

    Word Families: **objurgation** *n.*; **objurgatory** *adj.*

2. **enunciate**   [ɪˈnʌnsiˌet] *v.* to pronounce clearly; to utter; to claim

    He is always willing to **enunciate** his opinions about politics clearly.

    Word Families: **enunciation** *n*; **enunciator** *n.*; **enunciative** *adj.*

3. **exculpate**   [ˈɛkskʌlˌpeɪt] *v.* to prove that someone is not guilty of a crime or bad action

    Jack finally **exculpated** himself from a charge of theft in the bookstore.

Word Families: **exculpation** *n.*; **exculpatory** *n.*; **exculpatory** *adj.*

4. **extrapolate** [ɪkˈstræpəˌleɪt] *v.* to infer (something not known) from the know facts

   Extrapolating from his findings, he reckons about 80% of these deaths might be attributed to smoking.

   Word Families: **extrapolation** *n.*; **extrapolator** *n.*; **extrapolative** *adj.*

5. **facilitate** [fəˈsɪləˌteɪt] *v.* to make it possible or easier for something to happen

   I believe that this will **facilitate** our settlement of the matter.

   Word Families: **facilitation** *n.*; **facilitator** *n.*; **facilitative** *adj.*

6. **OBTRUDE** [ɑbˈtrud] *v.* to push oneself or one's ideas on others   **rhyming sound -ude**

   He didn't want to **obtrude** on her privacy.

   Word Families: **obtrusion** *n.*; **obtruder** *n.*; **obtrusive** *adj.*

7. **delude** [dɪˈlud] *v.* to make someone think something is not true

   Don't be deluded into thinking that we are out of danger yet.

   Word Families: **delusion** *n.*; **deluder** *n.*; **deludedly** *adv.*

8. **aptitude** [ˈæptɪˌtud] *n.* natural ability that makes it easy for you to do something well

   The girl showed a natural **aptitude** for painting.

   Word Families: **aptitudes** *n.pl.*

9. **lassitude** [ˈlæsɪˌtud] *n.* tiredness and lack of energy

   In general, symptoms of anemia include general fatigue and **lassitude**.

10. **rectitude** [ˈrektɪˌtud] *n.* a very moral and correct way of behaving

    The President is normally considered to be a man of the utmost moral **rectitude**.

SENTENCE COMPLETION

Choose one of the new words to complete each sentence below. Make changes if necessary.

| objurgate | enunciate | exculpate | extrapolate | facilitate |
| obtrude | delude | aptitude | lassitude | rectitude |

1. Forecasters can _____ the graph's future and then bet on the prediction.

2. Television _____ you into thinking you have experienced reality, when you haven't.

3. You should never _____ your opinions on others.

4. She is always willing to _____ her views to anyone who would listen.

5. It appears to me that some students have natural _____ for mathematics.

6. She was indignant with his presumption, self-satisfaction, and conscious _____.

7. The woman was _____ from the charge of murder.

8. A deadly _____ had taken hold of him.

9. Tom _____ her girl friend for being cruel to animals.

10. Thus, we shall obtain some illustrative materials which will _____ the understanding of the definition.

DEFINITION MATCHING

Choose one of the new words to match each definition below.

| objurgate | enunciate | exculpate | extrapolate | facilitate |
| obtrude | delude | aptitude | lassitude | rectitude |

11. natural ability to do something well   _____

12. a very moral and correct way of behaving   _____

13. tiredness and lack of energy   _____

14. infer something unknown from the known fact   _____

15. to make someone think that something is true _____

16. to scold somebody angrily _____

17. to make it possible for something to happen _____

18. to prove that someone is not guilty of a crime _____

19. to push oneself or one's ideas on others _____

20. to pronounce clearly; to utter; to claim _____

WRITING SENTENCES

Use each new word in the box to write an original sentence.

objurgate	enunciate	exculpate	extrapolate	facilitate
obtrude	delude	aptitude	lassitude	rectitude

21. _____
22. _____
23. _____
24. _____
25. _____
26. _____
27. _____
28. _____
29. _____
30. _____

UNIT 17

MEMORY TIPS:

Word building with Roots, Prefixes, and Suffixes:

arch	first, chief; as *oligarchy, anarchy, monarchy, hierarchy, patriarchy*
dis	apart, not; as *disputatious*
fort	strong; as *fortuitous*
ous, ious	characterized by; as *odious, fractious, facetious, fortuitous, disputatious*

NEW WORDS

odious	fractious	facetious	fortuitous	disputatious
oligarchy	anarchy	monarchy	hierarchy	patriarchy

1. ODIOUS ['oʊdiəs] *adj.* very unpleasant   **rhyming sound –ous**

Brad is certainly the most **odious** man I have ever seen.

Word Families: **odiousness** *n.*; **odiously** *adv.*

2. fractious ['frækʃəs] *adj.* easily upset or annoyed

That may make the world a little less **fractious**.

Word Families: **fractiousness** *n.*; **fractiously** *adv.*

3. facetious [fə'siʃəs] *adj.* trying to be funny in a way that is not appropriate

Does George Bush possess a disarming grin, or a **facetious** smirk?

Word Families: **facetiousness** *n.;* **facetiously** *adv.*

4. **fortuitous** [fɔr'tuɪtəs] *adj.* happening by chance

   His success is the result of a **fortuitous** combination of circumstances.

   Word Families: **fortuitousness** *n.;* **fortuitously** *adv.*

5. **disputatious** [ˌdɪspjə'teʃəs] *adj.* tending to dispute or argue without adequate cause

   She is the most **disputatious** girl in our class.

   Word Families: **disputatiousness** *n.;* **disputatiously** *adv.*

6. **OLIGARCHY** ['alɪˌgɑrki] *n.* government by a small group of people; state governed this way   **rhyming sound -archy**

   The small county was ruled by an **oligarchy** that had no concern for the welfare of the people.

   Word Families: **oligarchic** *adj.;* **oligarchical** *adj.;* **oligarchically** *adv.*

7. **anarchy** ['ænərki] *n.* lawlessness and disorder

   Civil war and famine sent the nation plunging into **anarchy**.

8. **monarchy** ['mɑnərki] *n.* government by or a state ruled by a sovereign

   By 1180 the native **Monarchy** of Ireland had gone to pieces.

   Word Families: **monarchies** *n.pl.*

9. **hierarchy** ['haɪəˌrɑrki] *n.* people or things arranged in a graded order

   There is a kind of social **hierarchy** even in this remote mountain village.

   Word Families: **hierarchization** *n;* **hierarchic** *adj.*

10. **patriarchy** ['peɪtriˌɑrki] *n.* a society in which men have most of the power

    That's not very different from what **patriarchy** always says about women.

    Word Families: **patriarchies** *n.pl.*

SENTENCE COMPLETION

Choose one of the new words to complete each sentence below. Make changes if necessary.

| odious | fractious | facetious | fortuitous | disputatious |
| oligarchy | anarchy | monarchy | hierarchy | patriarchy |

1. He had worked with the diverse, _____ Iraqi opposition.

2. There is a rigid _____ of power in that country.

3. There was a protest against imperialism and _____ in the region

4. This place has an _____ smell; something must be rotten.

5. The main cause of women's and children's oppression is _____.

6. There would be _____ if we had no police.

7. She kept interrupting our discussion with _____ remarks.

8. Thomas is a strong supporter of the _____.

9. No one likes to be associated with a _____ and arrogant person.

10. A series of _____ circumstances advanced her career.

DEFINITION MATCHING

Choose one of the new words to match each definition below.

| odious | fractious | facetious | fortuitous | disputatious |
| oligarchy | anarchy | monarchy | hierarchy | patriarchy |

11. lawlessness and disorder   _____

12. people or things arranged in a graded order   _____

13. trying to be funny in a way that is not appropriate   _____

14. happening by chance _____

15. a society in which men have most of the power _____

16. very unpleasant _____

17. government by a small group of people _____

18. government by or a state ruled by a sovereign _____

19. easily upset or annoyed _____

20. tending to argue without adequate cause _____

WRITING SENTENCES

Use each new word in the box to write an original sentence.

odious	fractious	facetious	fortuitous	disputatious
oligarchy	anarchy	monarchy	hierarchy	patriarchy

21. _____
22. _____
23. _____
24. _____
25. _____
26. _____
27. _____
28. _____
29. _____
30. _____

UNIT 18

MEMORY TIPS:

Word building with Roots, Prefixes, and Suffixes:

escent	becoming; as *putrescent, adolescent, opalescent*
ous, ious	characterized by; as *opprobrious, captious, horrendous, lecherous, mellifluous*

NEW WORDS

opalescent	ferment	fervent	putrescent	adolescent
opprobrious	captious	horrendous	lecherous	mellifluous

1. OPALESCENT [ˌoʊpəˈles(ə)nt] *adj.* iridescent like an opal   rhyming sound –ent

The beautiful girl turned her **opalescent** eyes on him.

Word Families: **opal** *n.*; **opalescence** *n.*

2. ferment [ˈfɜrˌment] *n.* commotion; unrest; *v.* undergo fermentation

The whole country has been in a state of political **ferment** for some months.

Word Families: **fermentation** *n.*; **fermentable** *adj.*

3. fervent [ˈfɜrv(ə)nt] *adj.* very enthusiastic and sincere about something

Their claims have been **fervently** denied by the committee.

Word Families: **fervency** *n.*; **fervently** *adv.*

4. putrescent [pju'tresənt] *adj.* decaying and smelling unpleasant

Some social reformers believe that the capitalist system is definitely **putrescent** and dying.

Word Families: **putrescence** *n.*; **putrescently** *adv.*

5. adolescent [ˌædə'les(ə)nt] *n. adj.* (person) between puberty and adulthood

An **adolescent** is often caught up in fantastic thoughts.

Word Families: **adolescents** *n.pl*; **adolescence** *n.*

6. OPPROBRIOUS [ə'probriəs] *adj.* deserving to be criticized severely for wrong one has done   rhyming sound -ous

He ransacked an extensive vocabulary in order to find **opprobrious** names to call her.

7. captious ['kæpʃəs] *adj.* intending to find fault and make criticism

His criticism was always **captious** and frivolous, never offering constructive suggestions.

Word Families: **captiousness** *n.*; **captiously** *adv.*

8. horrendous [hə'rendəs] *adj.* extremely bad or shocking

She described her trip as the most **horrendous** experience of her life.

Word Families: **horrendously** *adv.*

9. lecherous ['letʃərəs] *adj.* (of a man) having or showing excessive sexual desire

Mary felt that she could never avoid the **lecherous** eyes of her boss; therefore, she quit her office job.

Word Families: **lecherousness** *n.*; **lecherously** *adv.*

10. mellifluous [mə'lɪfluəs] *adj.* pleasant to listen to

The beautiful girl's voice was distinctive, soft, and **mellifluous**.

Word Families: **mellifluousness** *n.*; **mellifluously** *adv.*

SENTENCE COMPLETION

Choose one of the new words to complete each sentence below. Make changes if necessary.

| opalescent | ferment | fervent | putrescent | adolescent |
| opprobrious | captious | horrendous | lecherous | mellifluous |

1. It is highly important that an _____ girl should be able to confide to her mother.

2. It was a debate which aroused _____ ethical arguments.

3. The young people are becoming more and more _____ about what they wear nowadays.

4. It would be pointless to repeat the details of the most _____ crimes reported.

5. The sunset was making great splashes of fiery _____ across the sky.

6. The deserted house on the top of a small hill was _____ and scary.

7. The _____ old man who handed out candies to lure girls was finally arrested.

8. He is absolutely the most _____ man I have ever seen.

9. Nevertheless, the _____ in Japanese minds grew constantly more intense.

10. Soon the apartment was filled with _____ tones.

DEFINITION MATCHING

Choose one of the new words to match each definition below.

| opalescent | ferment | fervent | putrescent | adolescent |
| opprobrious | captious | horrendous | lecherous | mellifluous |

11. (of a man) having excessive sexual desire   _____

12. pleasant to listen to   _____

13. commotion; unrest _____

14. extremely bad or shocking _____

15. deserving to be criticized severely _____

16. iridescent like an opal _____

17. tending to find fault and make criticism _____

18. very enthusiastic and sincere about something _____

19. (person) between puberty and adulthood _____

20. decaying and smelling unpleasant _____

WRITING SENTENCES

Use each new word in the box to write an original sentence.

opalescent	ferment	fervent	putrescent	adolescent
opprobrious	captious	horrendous	lecherous	mellifluous

21. _____
22. _____
23. _____
24. _____
25. _____
26. _____
27. _____
28. _____
29. _____
30. _____

UNIT 19

MEMORY TIPS:

Word building with Roots, Prefixes, and Suffixes:

| ate | cause to be; as *originate, inculcate, instigate, litigate, immaculate* |
| con | together; as *condone* |

NEW WORDS

| originate | inculcate | instigate | litigate | immaculate |
| ozone | clone | condone | cyclone | silicone |

1. ORIGINATE [əˈrɪdʒə͵net] *v.* to come or bring into existence   rhyming sound –ate

The disease **originated** in Africa at the beginning of the century.

Word Families: **origination** *n.*; **originator** *n.*; **originative** *adj.*

2. inculcate [ˈɪnkʌl͵keɪt] *v.* to fix an idea or belief in someone's mind

Private banks, too, are trying novel approaches to help clients **inculcate** their values in succeeding generations.

Word Families: **inculcation** *n.*; **inculcator** *n.*

3. instigate [ˈɪnstɪ͵get] *v.* to cause to happen

The congress set up a special department to **instigate** the thing.

Word Families: **instigation** *n*; **instigator** *n.*

4. litigate ['lɪtɪˌgeɪt] *v.* to ask a court of law to make a decision

Both parties agreed to settle their claim out of court rather than **litigate**.

Word Families: **litigation** *n.*; **litigator** *n*

5. immaculate [ɪ'mækjələt] *adj.* completely clean or tidy; completely flawless

His 1988 Mercedes-Benz 300 E is in **immaculate** condition.

Word Families: **immaculacy** *n.*; **immaculateness** *n.*; **immaculately** *adv.*

6. OZONE ['oʊˌzoʊn] *n.* strong-smelling form of oxygen   **rhyming sound -one**

The **ozone** layer blocks some harmful rays which the sun gives off.

Word Families: **ozonic** *adj.*

7. clone [kloʊn] *n.* animal or plant produced artificially from the cells of another animal or plant; an exact copy of an animal or plant

A team of scientists from the Great Britain were the first to successfully **clone** an animal.

Word Families: **clonal** *adj.*

8. condone [kən'doʊn] *v.* to overlook or forgive (wrongdoing)

Terrorism can never be **condoned**.

Word Families: **condonation** *n.*; **condoner** *n.*

9. cyclone ['saɪˌkloʊn] *n.* a severe storm in which the winds spins in a circle

A **cyclone** in the Bay of Bengal is threatening the eastern Indian states.

Word Families: **cyclonic** *adj.*; **cyclonically** *adv.*

10. silicone ['sɪlɪˌkoʊn] *n.* substance made from silicon and used in lubricants or paints

NIH scientists were asked by Congress to study the safety of **silicone** breast implants.

Word Families: **silicon** *n.*

SENTENCE COMPLETION

Choose one of the new words to complete each sentence below. Make changes if necessary.

| originate | inculcate | instigate | litigate | immaculate |
| ozone | clone | condone | cyclone | silicone |

1. Did the council ever authorize the creation of a _____ army?

2. While many in China are fond of American culture, any attempt to _____ Chinese people with American values can be risky.

3. We can never _____ what he has done to the community.

4. As always, Michael was _____ dressed.

5. The _____ has resulted in the death of thousands of people.

6. It would not be worthwhile to _____ a nuclear attack.

7. What they find could provide clues to what might happen worldwide if _____ depletion continues.

8. Many species, for example, _____ in small populations.

9. A _____ filled version is available as an option for service at measuring points subject to strong vibration.

10. By contrast, the SEC is widely viewed as more prone to _____.

DEFINITION MATCHING

Choose one of the new words to match each definition below.

| originate | inculcate | instigate | litigate | immaculate |
| ozone | clone | condone | cyclone | silicone |

11. completely flawless _____

12. a storm in which the winds spins in a circle _____

13. to fix an idea or belief in someone's mind _____

14. substance made from silicon _____

15. to overlook or forgive (wrongdoing) _____

16. to come or bring into existence _____

17. an exact copy of an animal or plant _____

18. to ask a court of law to make a decision _____

19. strong-smelling form of oxygen _____

20. to cause to happen _____

WRITING SENTENCES

Use each new word in the box to write an original sentence.

originate	inculcate	instigate	litigate	immaculate
ozone	clone	condone	cyclone	silicone

21. _____
22. _____
23. _____
24. _____
25. _____
26. _____
27. _____
28. _____
29. _____
30. _____

UNIT 20

MEMORY TIPS:

Word building with Roots, Prefixes, and Suffixes:

able	able; as *palpable, viable, tractable, immutable, irreparable*
equi	equal; *as equinox*
im, ir	not; as *immutable, irreparable*
ortho	straight; as *orthodox*

NEW WORDS

palpable	viable	tractable	immutable	irreparable
paradox	jukebox	smallpox	equinox	orthodox

1. **PALPABLE** [ˈpælpəb(ə)l] *adj.* obvious or very easily noticed   **rhyming sound –able**

    There is a **palpable** difference in their ages.

    Word Families: **palpability** *n.;* **palpably** *adv.*

2. **viable** [ˈvaɪəb(ə)l] *adj.* able to be done, or worth doing

    Cash alone will not make Eastern Europe's banks **viable**.

    Word Families: **viability** *n.;* **viably** *adv.*

3. **tractable** [ˈtræktəb(ə)l] *adj.* easy to deal with

    The country's least **tractable** social problems are unemployment and crimes.

Word Families: **tractability** *n.;* **tractably** *adv.*

4. **immutable** [ɪˈmjutəb(ə)l] *adj.* impossible to change

There are no eternal and **immutable** principles of right and wrong.

Word Families: **immutability** *n.;* **immutably** *adv.*

5. **irreparable** [ɪˈrep(ə)rəb(ə)l] *adj.* extremely bad and cannot be repaired

The storm did **irreparable** damage to the small mountain village.

Word Families: **irreparability** *n.;* **irreparably** *adj.*

6. **PARADOX** [ˈperəˌdɑks] *n.* statement that seems self-contradictory but may be true
rhyming sound -ox

The **paradox** is that the region's most dynamic economies have the most primitive financial systems.

Word Families: **paradoxes** *n.pl.*

7. **jukebox** [ˈdʒukˌbɑks] *n.* coin operated machine that plays music

She got up, put some money in the **jukebox**, then sat back down

Word Families: **jukeboxes** *n.pl.*

8. **smallpox** [ˈsmɔlˌpɑks] *n.* contagious disease with blisters that leave scars

In 1742 he suffered a fatal attack of **smallpox**.

9. **equinox** [ˈekwɪˌnɑks] *n.* time of year when day and night are of equal length

The Autumnal **Equinox** is the best time for wheat-sowing.

Word Families: **equinoxes** *n.pl.*

10. **orthodox** [ˈɔrθəˌdɑks] *adj.* conforming to established views

These people are predominantly Russian **Orthodox** by religion.

Word Families: **orthodoxly** *adv.*

SENTENCE COMPLETION

Choose one of the new words to complete each sentence below. Make changes if necessary.

| palpable | viable | tractable | immutable | irreparable |
| paradox | jukebox | smallpox | equinox | orthodox |

1. The Nixon Administration deliberately withhold supplies from Israel to make it more _____ in negotiations.

2. The other point of intersection of equator and the ecliptic is called the Autumnal _____.

3. Flattery in its most _____ form had lost its force with her.

4. A new outbreak of _____ occurred in 1928.

5. His ideas about love and marriage are very _____.

6. The _____ ground out an incessant stream of pop music.

7. Our nature is not considered _____, either socially or biologically.

8. He has just made an _____ mistake.

9. Death itself is a _____, the end yet the beginning.

10. It is only their investment that makes the program economically _____.

DEFINITION MATCHING

Choose one of the new words to match each definition below.

| palpable | viable | tractable | immutable | irreparable |
| paradox | jukebox | smallpox | equinox | orthodox |

11. time of year day and night are the same length   _____

12. conforming to established views   _____

13. easy to deal with _____

14. contagious disease with blisters that leave scars _____

15. coin operated machine that plays music _____

16. obvious or very easily noticed _____

17. statement that seems self-contradictory _____

18. extremely bad and cannot be repaired _____

19. able to be done, or worth doing _____

20. impossible to change _____

WRITING SENTENCES

Use each new word in the box to write an original sentence.

palpable	viable	tractable	immutable	irreparable
paradox	jukebox	smallpox	equinox	orthodox

21. _____

22. _____

23. _____

24. _____

25. _____

26. _____

27. _____

28. _____

29. _____

30. _____

UNIT 21

MEMORY TIPS:

Word building with Roots, Prefixes, and Suffixes:

de	down, from; as *depravity*
dis	apart, away; as *disparity*
ity	state or quality; as *parity, brevity, alacrity, depravity, disparity*
morph	shape; as *amorphous*
ous	full of; as *parsimonious, arduous, amorphous, ambiguous, anonymous*

NEW WORDS

parity	brevity	alacrity	depravity	disparity
parsimonious	arduous	amorphous	ambiguous	anonymous

1. PARITY ['perəti] *n.* equality or equivalence   **rhyming sound –ity**

Women have yet to achieve wage or occupational **parity** in many fields.

Word Families: **parities** *n. pl.*

2. brevity ['brevəti] *n.* the use of a few words; the fact that something only lasts a short time

The **brevity** of the concert disappointed most of the audience.

3. alacrity [ə'lækrəti] *n.* promptness, speed, or eagerness

Although the man was very old, he still moved with **alacrity**.

4. **depravity** [dɪ'prævəti] *n.* behavior that is immoral or evil

   The patterns of human history mix decency and **depravity** in equal measure.

5. **disparity** [dɪ'sperəti] *n.* a difference between things

   The wide **disparity** between the rich and the poor is obvious in this country.

   Word Families: **disparities** *n.pl.*

6. **PARSIMONIOUS** ['bɔɪst(ə)rəs] *adj.* not willing to give or spend money   **rhyming sound -ious**

   At home, the man was churlish, **parsimonious,** and cruel to his daughter.

   Word Families: **parsimoniousness** *n.;* **parsimoniously** *adv.*

7. **arduous** ['ɑrdjuəs] *adj.* extremely difficult and involving a lot of effort

   The task was more **arduous** than he had imagined.

   Word Families: **arduousness** *n.;* **arduously** *adv.*

8. **amorphous** [ə'mɔrfəs] *adj.* with no clear shape, design, or structure

   No one could really understand his **amorphous** ideas.

   Word Families: **amorphousness** *n.;* **amorphously** *adv.*

9. **ambiguous** [æm'bɪgjuəs] *adj.* confusing or not definite

   The Foreign Minister's remarks clarify an **ambiguous** statement issued earlier this week.

   Word Families: **ambiguousness** *n;* **ambiguously** *adv.*

10. **anonymous** [ə'nɑnɪməs] *adj.* by someone whose name is unknown or withheld

    You can remain **anonymous** if you wish in this matter.

    Word Families: **anonymity** *n.;* **anonymously** *adv.*

SENTENCE COMPLETION

Choose one of the new words to complete each sentence below. Make changes if necessary.

| parity | brevity | alacrity | depravity | disparity |
| parsimonious | arduous | amorphous | ambiguous | anonymous |

1. The great _____ between the teams did not make for an entertaining game.

2. It is an _____ colorless or white powder.

3. Some of the codes are not shown for the purpose of _____.

4. Her claim was attended to with _____ by the insurance company.

5. The refugees made an _____ journey through the mountains.

6. The evil man led a life of total _____.

7. The government was ready to let the pound sink to _____ with the dollar if necessary.

8. We have received three _____ letters from Palestine to date, in addition to one suspicious package.

9. The wording in the agreement is so _____ that it leads to misinterpretations.

10. The millionaire's _____ nature did not permit him to enjoy any luxuries.

DEFINITION MATCHING

Choose one of the new words to match each definition below.

| parity | brevity | alacrity | depravity | disparity |
| parsimonious | arduous | amorphous | ambiguous | anonymous |

11. confusing or not definite   _____

12. by someone whose name is unknown   _____

13. extremely difficult and involving a lot of effort   _____

14. promptness, speed, or eagerness   _____

15. with no clear shape, design, or structure _____

16. equality or equivalence _____

17. not willing to give or spend money _____

18. behavior that is immoral or evil _____

19. the use of a few words _____

20. a difference between things _____

WRITING SENTENCES

Use each new word in the box to write an original sentence.

| parity | brevity | alacrity | depravity | disparity |
| parsimonious | arduous | amorphous | ambiguous | anonymous |

21. _____
22. _____
23. _____
24. _____
25. _____
26. _____
27. _____
28. _____
29. _____
30. _____

UNIT 22

MEMORY TIPS:

Word building with Roots, Prefixes, and Suffixes:

im	non; as *impunity*
ity	state or quality; as *paucity, probity, frugality, humility, impunity*
pro	forward, before; as *probity*

NEW WORDS

paucity	probity	frugality	humility	impunity
penury	fury	jury	mercury	perjury

1. **PAUCITY** ['pɔsəti] *n.* a small amount of something that is not enough rhyming sound –ity

   The **paucity** of fruit in this region was caused by the drought.

2. **probity** ['proʊbəti] *n.* a very moral and honest way of behaving

   A judge must be a person of unquestioned **probity**.

3. **frugality** [fru'gælətɪ] *n.* being thrifty and meager

   Certainly, we must not allow this **frugality** to cause a depression.

   Word Families: **frugal** *adj.;* **frugally** *adv.*

4. **humility** [hju'mɪləti] *n.* quality of being humble

Humility is a key virtue in a leader, too.

5. impunity [ɪmˈpjunəti] *n.* without punishment

Mr. Cook said future aggressors would be able to act with impunity if the objectives of the UN weren't met.

6. PENURY [ˈpɛnjʊri] *n.* the state of being extremely poor   **rhyming sound -icious**

Hardship and **penury** wore him out before his time.

7. fury [ˈfjʊri] *n.* a feeling of very strong anger

The innocent girl screamed and her face was distorted with **fury** and pain.

Word Families: **furies** *n.pl;* **furious** *adj.;* **furiously** *adv.*

8. jury [ˈdʒʊri] *n.* group of people sworn to deliver a verdict in a court of law

The **jury** found him guilty of manslaughter.

Word Families: **juries** *n.pl.*

9. mercury [ˈmɜrkjəri] *n.* silver liquid metal; **Mercury**, the planet near the sun

The liquid we can see in thermometers is **mercury**.

10. perjury [ˈpɜrdʒəri] *n.* the crime of lying when you give evidence in a court of law

This witness has committed **perjury**; therefore, no reliance can be placed on her evidence.

Word Families: **perjuries** *n.pl;* **perjurious** *adj.*

SENTENCE COMPLETION

Choose one of the new words to complete each sentence below. Make changes if necessary.

paucity	probity	frugality	humility	impunity
penury	fury	jury	mercury	perjury

1. No one can commit crimes with _____.

2. However, there is a _____ of research on the issue with Japanese subjects.

3. The _____ has not reached a verdict yet.

4. She felt that a wave of wild _____ overcame her.

5. Michael is truly a man with a deep sense of _____.

6. This is my prayer to thee, my lord - strike, strike at the root of _____ in my heart.

7. Just as companies' financial reports are audited, businesses should create a system to ensure _____.

8. The woman was sentenced to two years in prison for committing _____.

9. By _____ the woman managed to get along on her small salary.

10. _____ is the planet closest to the Sun.

DEFINITION MATCHING

Choose one of the new words to match each definition below.

paucity	probity	frugality	humility	impunity
penury	fury	jury	mercury	perjury

11. without punishment _____

12. silver liquid metal _____

13. a very moral and honest way of behaving _____

14. group of people sworn to deliver a verdict _____

15. the crime of lying when you give evidence _____

16. the state of being extremely poor _____

17. a small amount of something that is not enough _____

18. a feeling of very strong anger _____

19. being thrifty and meager _____

20. quality of being humble   _____

WRITING SENTENCES

Use each new word in the box to write an original sentence.

| paucity | probity | frugality | humility | impunity |
| penury | fury | jury | mercury | perjury |

21. _____
22. _____
23. _____
24. _____
25. _____
26. _____
27. _____
28. _____
29. _____
30. _____

UNIT 23

MEMORY TIPS:

Word building with Roots, Prefixes, and Suffixes:

---

ab	from, away; as *abnegation*
in	into, in, on; as *inventory*
ion	condition or action; as *perdition, adulation, abnegation, expiration, implication*

NEW WORDS

perdition	aspersion	abnegation	adulation	implication
peremptory	allegory	dilatory	inventory	perfunctory

1. **PERDITION** [pərˈdɪʃ(ə)n] *n.* spiritual ruin   **rhyming sound –ion**

   The man trembled whenever he thought of the **perdition**.

2. **aspersion** [əˈspɔːʒən] *n.* the making of defamatory remarks

   Carrie felt this to contain, in some way, an **aspersion** upon her ability.

3. **abnegation** [ˌæbnɪˈgeʃən] *n.* the denial and rejection of a doctrine or belief

   Only spontaneous love flowing with sincere generosity and self-**abnegation** can fertilize the soul of others.

4. **adulation** [ˌædʒəˈleɪʃ(ə)n] *n.* great praise or admiration, especially for someone who is famous

History abounds with great men worthy of **adulation** and emulation.

5. implication [ˌɪmplɪˈkeɪʃ(ə)n] *n.* a possible effect or result

The Attorney General was aware of the political **implication**s of his decision to prosecute the man for bribery.

Word Families: **implications** *n.pl.;* **implicational** *adj.*

6. PEREMPTORY [pəˈrempt(ə)ri] *adj.* speaking or behaving rather rudely as if you expect others to believe you immediately   **rhyming sound -ory**

In short, their position as it emerged in the three meetings with us was **peremptory** and unyielding

Word Families: **peremptoriness** *n.;* **peremptorily** *adv.*

7. allegory [ˈæləgəri] *n.* story with an underlying meaning as well as the literal one

"The Mysterious Stranger", his last book, is an **allegory** that suggests that life is in reality only a dream.

Word Families: **allegories** *n.pl;* **allegorist** *n.;* **allegorical** *adj.*

8. dilatory [ˈdɪləˌtɔri] *adj.* slow to do or decide something

It is not surprising that Toyota's response has been **dilatory** and inept, because crisis management in Japan is grossly undeveloped.

Word Families: **dilatoriness** *n.;* **dilatorily** *adv.*

9. inventory [ˈɪnvənˌtɔri] *n.* detailed list of goods and furnishings

The **inventory** showed that the store was overstocked.

Word Families: **inventories** *n.pl.*

10. perfunctory [pərˈfʌŋkt(ə)ri] *adj.* done without much effort or interest

He made some **perfunctory** remarks at the meeting.

Word Families: **perfunctoriness** *n.;* **perfunctorily** *adv.*

SENTENCE COMPLETION

Choose one of the new words to complete each sentence below. Make changes if necessary.

perdition	aspersion	abnegation	adulation	implication
peremptory	allegory	dilatory	inventory	perfunctory

1. Such _____ has become a popular tactic in these anti-political times.

2. His authority and, by _____, that of his management team is under threat.

3. This book is a kind of _____ of Latin American history.

4. It was their remarkable spirit that had prevented them from _____.

5. His _____ tone irritated almost everybody at the meeting.

6. Her recent novel was received with _____ by critics.

7. You might expect politicians to smooth things out when civil servants are being _____.

8. In the 19th century any reference to female sexuality was considered a vile _____.

9. The woman could not be negative or _____ about anything.

10. This product is in compliance with the Toxic Substance Control Act's _____ requirements

DEFINITION MATCHING

Choose one of the new words to match each definition below.

perdition	aspersion	abnegation	adulation	implication
peremptory	allegory	dilatory	inventory	perfunctory

11. a possible effect or result _____

12. detailed list of goods and furnishings _____

13. story with both underlying and literal meaning _____

14. done without much effort or interest _____

15. spiritual ruin _____

16. speaking or behaving rather rudely _____

17. slow to do or decide something _____

18. the denial and rejection of a doctrine or belief _____

19. great praise or admiration _____

20. the making of defamatory remarks _____

WRITING SENTENCES

Use each new word in the box to write an original sentence.

perdition	aspersion	abnegation	adulation	implication
peremptory	allegory	dilatory	inventory	perfunctory

21. _____
22. _____
23. _____
24. _____
25. _____
26. _____
27. _____
28. _____
29. _____
30. _____

UNIT 24

MEMORY TIPS:

Word building with Roots, Prefixes, and Suffixes:

ious, ous	characterized by; as *perfidious, tenuous, momentous, ominous, vociferous*
inter	between, among; as *interfuse*
per	through, intensive; as *perfidious, peruse*

NEW WORDS

perfidious	tenuous	momentous	ominous	vociferous
peruse	fuse	muse	abuse	interfuse

1. PERFIDIOUS [pər'fɪdiəs] *adj.* not able to be trusted   **rhyming sound –ous**

This is a **perfidious** crime of aggression not only against this country but also against the freedom and independence of all nations

Word Families: **perfidiousness** *n.*; **perfidiously** *adv.*

2. tenuous ['tɛnjuəs] *adj.* weak and likely to change

This decision puts the President in a somewhat **tenuous** position.

Word Families: **tenuousness** *n.*; **tenuously** *adv.*

3. momentous [moʊ'mɛntəs] *adj.* very important

The past five years have been among the most **momentous** in the history of science and technology.

Word Families: **momentousness** *n.;* **momentously** *adv.*

4. **ominous** ['ɑmɪnəs] *adj.* threatening; indicating evil or harm

There are already **ominous** signs in the air for the industry.

Word Families: **ominousness** *n.;* **ominously** *adj.*

5. **vociferous** [voʊ'sɪfərəs] *adj.* loud; shouting

A smaller programme ensures that less **vociferous** students do not get left behind.

Word Families: **vociferousness** *n.;* **vociferously** *adv..*

6. **PERUSE** [pə'ruz] *v.* to read something   rhyming sound -use

You should **peruse** the terms and conditions carefully before using any service.

Word Families: **peruser** *n.*

7. **fuse** [fjuːz] *n.* safety device for electric circuit; *v.* to join; to unite by melting

The conflict further became the **fuse** of the World War II.

Word Families: **fusion** *n.;* **fuseless** *adj.*

8. **muse** [mjuz] *v.* to ponder quietly; *n.* force or person that inspires a creative artist

She once **mused** that she would have been the First Lady of the United States had she had the chance to go to college with the President.

9. **abuse** [ə'bjus] *v.* to use wrongly; to ill-treat violently; *n.* wrong use; ill-treatment

"There was no **abuse**, name-calling, threats, punishment, bans or dismissals," he said.

10. **interfuse** [ˌɪntə'fjuːz] *v.* to mingle, blend, or fuse thoroughly

All these mechanisms can interact and **interfuse** and form intelligently and naturally operating mechanisms.

Word Families: **interfusion** *n.*

SENTENCE COMPLETION

Choose one of the new words to complete each sentence below. Make changes if necessary.

| perfidious | tenuous | momentous | ominous | vociferous |
| peruse | fuse | muse | abuse | interfuse |

1. The second question is less _____, but more baffling.

2. He was a _____ opponent of Conservatism.

3. The cultural and historical links between the many provinces were seen to be very _____.

4. Anyone can _____ the details of software for whatever reason he or she likes.

5. Your _____ gossip is malicious and dangerous.

6. He spoke _____ of the world facing a war in Europe and possibly something greater.

7. This is the right _____ for the refrigerator.

8. The man alleged that he was verbally _____ by other soldiers.

9. We had a heated discussion on the _____ of traditional library and digital library.

10. Plenty of women have been both lover, and _____ to famous artists, like Picasso..

DEFINITION MATCHING

Choose one of the new words to match each definition below.

| perfidious | tenuous | momentous | ominous | vociferous |
| peruse | fuse | muse | abuse | interfuse |

11. force or person that inspires a creative artist   _____

12. to mingle, blend, or fuse thoroughly _____

13. not able to be trusted _____

14. wrong use; ill-treatment _____

15. to join; to unite by melting _____

16. weak and likely to change _____

17. loud; shouting _____

18. to read something _____

19. threatening; indicating evil or harm _____

20. very important _____

WRITING SENTENCES

Use each new word in the box to write an original sentence.

perfidious	tenuous	momentous	ominous	vociferous
peruse	fuse	muse	abuse	interfuse

21. _____

22. _____

23. _____

24. _____

25. _____

26. _____

27. _____

28. _____

29. _____

30. _____

UNIT 25

MEMORY TIPS:

Word building with Roots, Prefixes, and Suffixes:

co	together; as *coalition*
dis	not; as *dissuasive*
ion	act of; as *petition, rendition, tuition, acquisition, coalition*
ive	relating to; as *pervasive, abrasive, dissuasive, evasive, persuasive*
pet	seek; as *petition*
per	through, intensive; as *pervasive, persuasive*

NEW WORDS

pervasive	abrasive	dissuasive	evasive	persuasive
petition	rendition	acquisition	coalition	intuition

1. PERVASIVE [pər'veɪsɪv] *adj.* spreading right through something **rhyming sound –asive**

The bigger, more **pervasive** problem is on the demand side.

Word Families: **pervasiveness** *n.;* **pervasively** *adv.*

2. abrasive [ə'breɪsɪv] *adj.* harsh and unpleasant in manner; *n.* substance for cleaning and polishing by rubbing

Jack's abrasive manner has won him an unenviable notoriety.

Word Families: **abrasives** *n.pl.*; **abrasiveness** *n.*

3. dissuasive [dɪˈsweɪsɪv] *adj.* deterring somebody by persuasion from doing something

It seems that all the evidence to the contrary is not entirely **dissuasive**.

Word Families: **dissuasiveness** *n;* **dissuasion** *n.*

4. evasive [iˈveɪsɪv] *adj.* not talking or answering questions in a honest way

He was **evasive** about the details of his recent meeting with the President.

Word Families: **evasiveness** *n.;* **evasively** *adv.*

5. persuasive [pərˈsweɪsɪv] *adj.* good at making people agree to do or believe

The mayor's arguments in favor of a new school are very **persuasive**.

Word Families: **persuasiveness** *n.;* **persuasively** *adv.*

6. PETITION [pəˈtɪʃ(ə)n] *n.* formal request signed by many people; *v.* present a petition to
rhyming sound -ition

They recently presented the city government with a **petition** signed by 1000 people.

Word Families: **petitioner** *n.;* **petitionary** *adj.*

7. rendition [renˈdɪʃ(ə)n] *n.* performance; translation

"He's delightful, delightful," he went on, giving the commonplace **rendition** of approval which such men know.

8. acquisition [ˌækwɪˈzɪʃ(ə)n] *n.* thing acquired; act of getting

He devoted almost all his time to the **acquisition** of knowledge.

9. coalition [ˌkoʊəˈlɪʃ(ə)n] *n.* temporary alliance between political parties

It took five months for the **coalition** to agree on and publish a medium-term economic program.

10. intuition [ˌɪntuˈɪʃ(ə)n] *n.* instinctive knowledge or insight without conscious reasoning

Her **intuition** was telling her that something was wrong.

Word Families: **intuitions** *n.pl..;* **intuitional** *adj.*

SENTENCE COMPLETION

Choose one of the new words to complete each sentence below. Make changes if necessary.

pervasive	abrasive	dissuasive	evasive	persuasive
petition	rendition	acquisition	coalition	intuition

1. Mary looked at the man closely to see if his _____ was intentional.

2. His _____ argument made everybody feel confused at the meeting.

3. The evidence was not really _____ enough to convince the jury.

4. Digital wireless networks are still not _____ today.

5. I had an _____ that I would find you.

6. He had been opposed by a _____ of about 50 civil rights, women's and Latino organizations.

7. She lifted her voice during her _____ of the classic opera song.

8. If another _____ opportunity comes up, we would certainly not rule it out.

9. Many colleagues regard Summers as _____, but Greenspan sounds affectionate.

10. His lawyers filed a _____ for all charges to be dropped.

DEFINITION MATCHING

Choose one of the new words to match each definition below.

pervasive	abrasive	dissuasive	evasive	persuasive
petition	rendition	acquisition	coalition	intuition

11. formal request signed by many people   _____

12. performance; translation   _____

13. harsh and unpleasant in manner   _____

14. thing acquired; act of getting   _____

15. instinctive knowledge   _____

16. good at making people to do or believe   _____

17. deterring somebody by persuasion from doing _____

18. temporary alliance between political parties _____

19. not talking or answering in a honest way _____

20. spreading right through something   _____

WRITING SENTENCES

Use each new word in the box to write an original sentence.

pervasive	abrasive	dissuasive	evasive	persuasive
petition	rendition	acquisition	coalition	intuition

21. _____
22. _____
23. _____
24. _____
25. _____
26. _____
27. _____
28. _____
29. _____
30. _____

UNIT 26

MEMORY TIPS:

Word building with Roots, Prefixes, and Suffixes:

com	together; as *comprehend*
epi	upon, close to, over, after, altered; as *epistemic*
ic	of, like; as *polemic, alchemic, endemic, academic, epistemic*
port	carry, bring; as *portend*

NEW WORDS

polemic	endemic	systemic	epidemic	epistemic
portend	blend	amend	apprehend	reprehend

1. **POLEMIC** [pəˈlemɪk] *n.* argument about doctrines   **rhyming sound –emic**

    But underlying his **polemic** lay a disapproval of manufacturers foisting goods on consumers who did not really need them.

    Word Families: **polemics** *n. pl.;* **polemicist** *n.;* **polemical** *adj.*

2. **endemic** [enˈdemɪk] *adj.* very common, or strongly established in a place

    Food shortages and starvation are **endemic** in certain parts of the world.

    Word Families: **endemicity** *n.;* **endemism** *n.;* **endemically** *adv.*

3. **systemic** [sɪˈstemɪk] *adj.* affecting all of something; affecting your whole body

The national economy is currently locked in a **systemic** crisis.

Word Families: **systemically** *adv.*

4. **epidemic** [ˌepɪ'demɪk] *n.* widespread occurrence of a disease

    A flu **epidemic** is sweeping through southwest region of the country.

    Word Families: **epidemics** *n. pl.*

5. **epistemic** [ˌɛpɪ'stimɪk] *adj.* relating to knowledge

    A second version of the classical approach would focus on the **epistemic** goal of having justified or rational beliefs.

    Word Families: **epistemically** *adj.*

6. **PORTEND** [pɔr'tend] *n.* to be a sign or warning that something will happen   **rhyming sound -end**

    The change did not **portend** a basic improvement in social conditions.

7. **blend** [blend] *v.* to mix or mingle; *n.* mixture

    The New City Centre offers a subtle **blend** of traditional charm with modern amenities.

8. **amend** [ə'mend] *v.* to make changes to a document or law agreement

    The President has agreed to **amend** the constitution and allow multi-party elections.

    Word Families: **amendment** *n.;* **amender** *n.;* **amendable** *adj.*

9. **apprehend** [ˌæprɪ'hend] *v.* to arrest someone; to understand something

    The police have **apprehended** the killer of the old woman.

10. **reprehend** [ˌrɛprɪ'hɛnd] *v.* to criticize or reprove somebody or something

    His conduct deserves to be **reprehended**.

SENTENCE COMPLETION

Choose one of the new words to complete each sentence below. Make changes if necessary.

polemic	endemic	systemic	epidemic	epistemic
portend	blend	amend	apprehend	reprehend

1. Third, containing _____ financial risk is not enough to restore growth.

2. Street crime is virtually _____ in large cities in the United States.

3. Here a social communicational device is treated as a type of _____ standard.

4. Mr. Gates avoided raising the rhetorical ante with the former KGB officer, preferring instead to laugh off the _____.

5. Sometimes small events can _____ great changes.

6. The sea and sky seemed to _____ on the horizon.

7. The little mountain village was smitten by an _____.

8. The girl was severely _____ for torturing the little cat.

9. Only now can I begin to _____ the power of these forces.

10. Government has no firm position on how to _____ the two electoral methods.

DEFINITION MATCHING

Choose one of the new words to match each definition below.

polemic	endemic	systemic	epidemic	epistemic
portend	blend	amend	apprehend	reprehend

11. to arrest someone   _____

12. to criticize or reprove somebody or something   _____

13. argument about doctrines   _____

14. to make changes to a document or agreement   _____

15. to mix or mingle   _____

16. very common, or strongly established in a place _____

17. to be a sign that something will happen _____

18. widespread occurrence of a disease _____

19. relating to knowledge _____

20. affecting all of something _____

WRITING SENTENCES

Use each new word in the box to write an original sentence.

| polemic | endemic | systemic | epidemic | epistemic |
| portend | blend | amend | apprehend | reprehend |

21. _____

22. _____

23. _____

24. _____

25. _____

26. _____

27. _____

28. _____

29. _____

30. _____

UNIT 27

MEMORY TIPS:

Word building with Roots, Prefixes, and Suffixes:

con	together; as *concept*
in	not; as *inept*
ious	characterized by; as *precocious, spacious, specious, atrocious, ferocious*
inter	between, among; as *intercept*

NEW WORDS

precept	concept	incept	inept	intercept
precocious	spacious	specious	atrocious	ferocious

1. **PRECEPT** ['pri,sept] *n.* rule of behavior   **rhyming sound –ept**

   Armed with certain **precepts**, a number of doctors may slip into deceptive practices.

   Word Families: **precepts** *n. pl.;* **perceptive** *adj.*

2. **concept** ['kɒnsept] *n.* abstract or general idea

   She added that the **concept** of arranged marriages is misunderstood in the west.

   Word Families: **concepts** *n.pl.*

3. incept [In'sept] *v.* to begin; to start something

The training program has been successful since its **inception**.

Word Families: **inception** *n. pl.;* **inceptor** *n.*

4. inept [I'nept] *n.* clumsy; lacking skill

Generally speaking, David Campbell was an **inept** politician.

Word Families: **ineptitude** *n;* **ineptness** *n.;* **ineptly** *adv..*

5. intercept [ˌIntər'sept] *v.* to stop, catch or take control of somebody or something

The small country plans to **intercept** foreign missiles when it is necessary.

Word Families: **interception** *n.;* **interceptive** *adj.*

6. PRECOCIOUS [prɪ'koʊʃəs] *adj.* having developed or matured too early or too soon

rhyming sound -icious

Despite her **precocious** talent for mathematics, she failed it at the graduation test.

Word Families: **precociousness** *n.;* **precocity** *n.;* **precociously** *adv.*

7. spacious ['speɪʃəs] *adj.* having a large capacity or area

They have moved to a more **spacious** residence on the west side of Vancouver.

Word Families: **spaciousness** *n.;* **spaciously** *adv.*

8. specious ['spiʃəs] *adj.* seeming to be true but in fact wrong

An international regulator is better positioned to resist these often **specious** arguments.

9. atrocious [ə'troʊʃəs] *adj.* very evil or cruel; very unpleasant

The judge said he the man had committed **atrocious** crimes against women.

Word Families: **atrociousness** *n;* **atrociously** *adv..*

10. ferocious [fə'roʊʃəs] *adj.* savagely fierce or cruel

Mr. Obama can also fairly complain that he has faced **ferocious** opposition.

Word Families: **ferociousness** *n.;* **ferociously** *adv.*

SENTENCE COMPLETION

Choose one of the new words to complete each sentence below. Make changes if necessary.

precept	concept	incept	inept	intercept
precocious	spacious	specious	atrocious	ferocious

1. A high ceiling creates a feeling of _____.

2. It is unlikely that the President was convinced by such _____ arguments.

3. Since its _____ in 1975, our export business has enjoyed tremendous growth.

4. He felt confronted by the most _____ suffering he had ever known.

5. Freud first mentioned this _____ in his paper "On Narcissism".

6. Many of her letters were _____ by the Secret Service.

7. It occurs to me that example is always more efficacious than _____.

8. She was _____ and lacked the skills to govern such an international organization.

9. The police had to deal with some of the most _____ violence in the city.

10. Thirty years later, this _____ youth was to be the first President of the United States.

DEFINITION MATCHING

Choose one of the new words to match each definition below.

precept	concept	incept	inept	intercept
precocious	spacious	specious	atrocious	ferocious

11. having developed or matured too early   _____

12. seeming to be true but in fact wrong _____

13. rule of behavior _____

14. stop or catch somebody or something _____

15. savagely fierce or cruel _____

16. abstract or general idea _____

17. very evil or cruel; very unpleasant _____

18. having a large capacity or area _____

19. to begin; to start something _____

20. clumsy; lacking skill _____

WRITING SENTENCES

Use each new word in the box to write an original sentence.

precept	concept	incept	inept	intercept
precocious	spacious	specious	atrocious	ferocious

21. _____

22. _____

23. _____

24. _____

25. _____

26. _____

27. _____

28. _____

29. _____

30. _____

UNIT 28

MEMORY TIPS:

Word building with Roots, Prefixes, and Suffixes:

ate	Verb: cause to be; as *preponderate, prate, profligate, elaborate, repudiate*
con	together; as *consolidate, conservative*
extra	out of, beyond; as *extrapolate*
ive	relating to; as *prerogative, correlative, derivative, figurative, preservative*
pre	before; as *preservative*

NEW WORDS

preponderate	prate	profligate	elaborate	repudiate
prerogative	correlative	derivative	figurative	preservative

1. **PREPONDERATE** [prɪˈpɑndəˌret] *v.* to be greater in force, amount or influence   **rhyming sound –ate**

   Therefore, shaping about innovation psychology should not **preponderate** over the principle with practice determining theory.

   Word Families: **preponderance** *n.*

2. **prate**   [preɪt] *v.* to talk in a silly way for a long time; to babble

   I know the age better than you do, though you will **prate** about it so tediously.

3. profligate ['prɑflɪgɪt] *adj.* wasteful

The young millionaire's **profligate** lifestyle resulted in bankruptcy.

Word Families: **profligacy** *n.;* **profligately** *adj.*

4. elaborate [ɪ'læb(ə)rət] *v.* to give more details about something; *n.* very detailed and complicated

Elaborate efforts at the highest level have been made to conceal the problem.

Word Families: **elaboration** *n.;* **elaborately** *adj.*

5. repudiate [rɪ'pjudi,eɪt] *v.* to say formally that something is not true

The Prime Minister has **repudiated** racist remarks made by a member of the Conservative Party.

6. PREROGATIVE [prɪ'rɑgətɪv] *n.* privilege or right   rhyming sound -ative

This **prerogative** is left to the 1,000 or more authorized business schools spread throughout the country.

Word Families: **prerogatives** *n.pl.*

7. correlative [kə'relətɪv] *adj.* being placed in a mutual relationship

Time is **correlative** with speed.

Word Families: **correlativity** *n.;* **correlation** *n.; re* **correlatively** *adv.*

8. derivative [dɪ'rɪvətɪv] *adj.* words, idea, etc. derived from another; *n.* something that has developed from something else

This isn't an entirely new car, but a new **derivative** of the Citroen XM.

9. figurative ['fɪgərətɪv] *adj.* (of language) abstract, imaginative, or symbolic

Europe, with Germany literally and **figuratively** at its centre, is still at the start of a remarkable transformation.

10. preservative [prɪ'zɜrvətɪv] *n.* chemical that prevents decay

Salt is a **preservative** for meat or fish.

SENTENCE COMPLETION

Choose one of the new words to complete each sentence below. Make changes if necessary.

| preponderate | prate | profligate | elaborate | repudiate |
| prerogative | correlative | derivative | figurative | preservative |

1. Similarly Americans have been _____ in the handling of mineral resources.

2. However, the Citizens opinion does not necessarily _____ that proposition.

3. His task was to _____ policies which would make a market economy compatible with a clean environment

4. Ethnic Chinese _____ in the population of Singapore.

5. Making such decisions is not the sole _____ of managers.

6. If the hen does not _____, she will not lay.

7. This kind of wood is treated with _____ to prevent decay.

8. A lot of what you see in stand-up comedy today is very _____.

9. No one was doing realistic _____ art other than cowboys and Indians.

10. The price includes the _____ fees to exporting all the cargos.

DEFINITION MATCHING

Choose one of the new words to match each definition below.

| preponderate | prate | profligate | elaborate | repudiate |
| prerogative | correlative | derivative | figurative | preservative |

11. wasteful   _____

12. privilege or right   _____

13. to be greater in force, amount or influence _____

14. chemical that prevents decay _____

15. (of language) abstract, imaginative, or symbolic _____

16. to talk in a silly way for a long time _____

17. words, idea, etc. derived from another _____

18. to say formally that something is wrong _____

19. being placed in a mutual relationship _____

20. to give more details about something _____

WRITING SENTENCES

Use each new word in the box to write an original sentence.

| preponderate | prate | profligate | elaborate | repudiate |
| prerogative | correlative | derivative | figurative | preservative |

21. _____
22. _____
23. _____
24. _____
25. _____
26. _____
27. _____
28. _____
29. _____
30. _____

UNIT 29

MEMORY TIPS:

Word building with Roots, Prefixes, and Suffixes:

dia	across, through; as *diagnosis*
ic	of, like; as *prolific, horrific, specific, terrific, colorific*
pro	before; as *prognosis, prolific*

NEW WORDS

prognosis	hypnosis	diagnosis	scoliosis	tuberculosis
prolific	horrific	specific	terrific	colorific

1. **PROGNOSIS** [prɑg'noʊsɪs] *n.* doctor's forecast about an illness; any forecast **rhyming sound –osis**

   The doctor's **prognosis** was that Laurence might walk within 12 months.

   Word Families: **prognoses** *n. pl.*

2. **hypnosis** [hɪp'noʊsɪs] *n.* artificially induced state of relaxation in which the mind is more than usually receptive to suggestion

   This is the **hypnosis** technique which can help self-healing.

   Word Families: **hypnoses** *n. pl.;* **hypnotic** *adj.;* **hypnotically** *adv.*

3. **diagnosis** [ˌdaɪəg'noʊsɪs] *n.* a statement about what disease someone has

The doctor made his **diagnosis** after studying the patient's symptoms.

Word Families: **diagnoses** *n. pl.;* **diagnostic** *adj.*

4. scoliosis [ˌskoʊlɪˈoʊsɪs] *n.* an excessive sideways curvature of the human spine

    Progression of **scoliosis** can occur in patients who experience rapid growth.

    Word Families: **scoliotic** *adj.*

5. tuberculosis [tʊˌbɜrkjəˈloʊsɪs] *n.* a serious infectious disease affecting your lungs

    HIV infection reduces the body immunity against mycobacterium **tuberculosis**.

6. PROLIFIC [prəˈlɪfɪk] *adj.* productive; fertile   rhyming sound -ific

    Mice are **prolific** breeders.

    Word Families: **prolificacy** *n.;* **prolificness** *n.;* **prolifically** *adv.*

7. horrific [həˈrɪfɪk] *adj.* so shocking that upsets you

    President Obama also called it a "**horrific** and cowardly attack."

    Word Families: **horrifically** *adv.*

8. specific [spəˈsɪfɪk] *adj.* exact and detailed

    He would not discuss whether any **specific** regulatory demands might be deal-breakers.

    Word Families: **specificity** *n.;* **specificness** *n.;* **specifically** *adv.*

9. terrific [təˈrɪfɪk] *adj.* very good or interesting

    The company tried to tell customers they were still getting a "**terrific** value."

    Word Families: **terrifically** *adv.*

10. colorific [ˌkʌləˈrɪfɪk] *adj.* producing or giving color to something

    We should pay special attention to the **colorific** configuration of the bathroom due to its limited space.

SENTENCE COMPLETION

Choose one of the new words to complete each sentence below. Make changes if necessary.

| prognosis | hypnosis | diagnosis | scoliosis | tuberculosis |
| prolific | horrific | specific | terrific | colorific |

1. The plain radiograph of the spine demonstrated mild _____.

2. Mary Jones is a _____ writer of children's stories.

3. The _____ for the economy is uncertain.

4. The error message is not _____, but at least you know where it is.

5. The film showed the most _____ murder scenes we had ever seen.

6. _____ was deferred pending further assessment.

7. All of a sudden there was a _____ bang and a flash of smoke.

8. The _____ features reflect the local culture from historic evolvement, ethical mentality, religion, etc.

9. Some people claim that they have been cured of smoking by _____.

10. _____ is a curable disease.

DEFINITION MATCHING

Choose one of the new words to match each definition below.

| prognosis | hypnosis | diagnosis | scoliosis | tuberculosis |
| prolific | horrific | specific | terrific | colorific |

11. a serious infectious disease affecting your lungs _____

12. so shocking that upsets you _____

13. producing or giving color to something _____

14. a sideways curvature of the human spine _____

15. very good or interesting _____

16. artificially induced state of relaxation _____

17. exact and detailed _____

18. a statement about what disease someone has _____

19. productive; fertile _____

20. doctor's forecast of an illness; any forecast _____

WRITING SENTENCES

Use each new word in the box to write an original sentence.

| prognosis | hypnosis | diagnosis | scoliosis | tuberculosis |
| prolific | horrific | specific | terrific | colorific |

21. _____
22. _____
23. _____
24. _____
25. _____
26. _____
27. _____
28. _____
29. _____
30. _____

UNIT 30

MEMORY TIPS:

Word building with Roots, Prefixes, and Suffixes:

ate	Verb: cause to be; as *prognosticate, implicate, eradicate, reiterate, relegate, propitiate, deviate, initiate, mediate, differentiate*
in	in, into, on; as *implicate*
re	back, again; as *reiterate, relegate*

NEW WORDS

prognosticate	implicate	reiterate	relegate	eradicate
propitiate	deviate	initiate	mediate	differentiate

1. **PROGNOSTICATE** [prɑg'nɑstɪˌket] *v.* to make a prediction about; to tell in advance
   rhyming sound –ate

   It has long been fashionable for visionaries to **prognosticate** about the direction technology.

   Word Families: **prognosticator** *n.;* **prognosticatory** *adj.*

2. **implicate** ['ɪmplɪˌkeɪt] *v.* to indicate indirectly; to suggest something

   His investigation would eventually **implicate** his brother in the crime.

   Word Families: **implication** *n.;* **implicatively** *adv.*

3. reiterate [ri'ɪtə,reɪt] *v.* to repeat something in order to emphasize it

The Government deems it necessary to **reiterate** its position and policy on the these matters.

4. relegate ['relə,geɪt] *v.* to banish; to assign to a inferior position

Some scientists **relegate** parapsychology to the sphere of quackery.

5. eradicate [ɪ'rædɪ,keɪt] *v.* to get rid of something completely

Although these substances would not **eradicate** the AIDS virus, still they can effectively control their reproduction.

6. PROPITIATE [proʊ'pɪʃi,eɪt] *v.* to appease; to win the favor of   rhyming sound -iate

McKinley was eager to **propitiate** the agrarian Middle West after his close victory over Bryan in 1896.

Word Families: **propitiator** *n.*; **propitiatory** *adj.*

7. deviate ['divi,eɪt] *v.* to depart from one's previous behavior; to differ from others in thoughts or beliefs

His statement seemed slightly to **deviate** from the truth.

8. initiate [ɪ'nɪʃi,eɪt] *v.* to begin

The military preparations that have occurred do not indicate that any party intends to **initiate** hostilities.

Word Families: **initiation** *n.*; **initiatory** *adj.*

9. mediate ['midi,eɪt] *v.* to try to end a disagreement between two parties

They may be able to **mediate** between parties with different interests.

Word Families: **mediation** *n*; **mediator** *n.*; **mediatory** *adj.*

10. differentiate [,dɪfə'rɛnʃi,et] *v.* to mark as different

A child may not be able to **differentiate** between his imagination and the real world.

Word Families: **differentiation** *n.*; **differentiator** *n.*

SENTENCE COMPLETION

Choose one of the new words to complete each sentence below. Make changes if necessary.

| prognosticate | implicate | reiterate | relegate | eradicate |
| propitiate | deviate | initiate | mediate | differentiate |

1. We can no longer _____ Afghanistan to the bottom of our priority list.

2. From very early on he believed a military revolution was necessary and he has never _____ from that ideological path.

3. We must take this good opportunity to fight an excellent _____ battle.

4. It would be very hard to _____ about the company's earnings next year.

5. At this stage the little baby cannot _____ one person from another.

6. Our trip was _____ by the manager of the community centre.

7. These scandals _____ many of the country's most powerful leaders.

8. The ceremony was believed to encourage fertility, demonstrate piety, and _____ the gods.

9. His wife had a fight with his mother; he tried every means to _____ between them.

10. I continue to _____ that students are expected to be respectful when learning at school.

DEFINITION MATCHING

Choose one of the new words to match each definition below.

| prognosticate | implicate | reiterate | relegate | eradicate |
| propitiate | deviate | initiate | mediate | differentiate |

11. to get rid of something completely   _____

12. to mark as different   _____

13. to appease; to win the favor of _____

14. to try to end a disagreement between two parties _____

15. to begin _____

16. to make a prediction about _____

17. to repeat _____

18. to differ from others in thoughts or beliefs _____

19. to indicate indirectly _____

20. to banish; to assign to a inferior position _____

WRITING SENTENCES

Use each new word in the box to write an original sentence.

prognosticate	implicate	reiterate	relegate	eradicate
propitiate	deviate	initiate	mediate	differentiate

21. _____
22. _____
23. _____
24. _____
25. _____
26. _____
27. _____
28. _____
29. _____
30. _____

UNIT 31

MEMORY TIPS:

Word building with Roots, Prefixes, and Suffixes:

cid	cut, kill; as *incident*
co	together; as *coincident*
in	in, into, on; as *incident*
pro	before; as *protocol, provident*

NEW WORDS

protocol	menthol	alcohol	parasol	cholesterol
provident	diffident	evident	incident	coincident

1. **PROTOCOL** ['proʊtə,kɔl] *n.* rules of behavior for formal occasions **rhyming sound –ol**

    Climate change negotiators are trying to come up with a workable draft document to replace the 1997 Kyoto **Protocol**.

    Word Families: **protocols** *n. pl.*

2. **menthol** ['men,θɑl] *n.* a substance that smells and tastes like mint

    Menthol cigarettes are almost produced entirely in the US.

3. **alcohol** ['ælkə,hɔl] *n.* intoxicating drinks generally

    Thomas has finally got rid of his addiction to **alcohol**.

Word Families: **alcoholic** *adj.*

4. parasol ['pærə,sɔl] *n.* umbrella-like sunshade

She smiled beneath the **parasol** at the soft warmth of the day.

Word Families: **parasols** *n. pl.*

5. cholesterol [kə'lestərɑl] *n.* fatty substance found in animal tissue, an excess of which can cause heart disease

Eating garlic can significantly reduce **cholesterol** in the blood.

6. PROVIDENT ['prɑvɪdənt] *adj.* thrifty; showing foresight   **rhyming sound -icious**

The housing **provident** fund system needs to be reformed immediately to meet the needs of the buyers.

Word Families: **providence** *n.;* **providently** *adv.*

7. diffident ['dɪfɪdənt] *adj.* shy

The beautiful girl has a politely **diffident** manner.

Word Families: **diffidence** *n.;* **diffidently** *adv.*

8. evident ['evɪdənt] *adj.* easy to see, notice, or understand

The spokesman made it **evident** that no compromise was yet in sight.

Word Families: **evidence** *n.;* **evidently** *adv.*

9. incident ['ɪnsɪdənt] *n.* something that happens; event involving violence

In a statement, the President Bush said he 'was shocked and deeply saddened' by the **incident**.

Word Families: **incidents** *n.pl.*

10. coincident [ko'ɪnsɪdənt] *adj.* in agreement

The results were **coincident** with the calculated data and the thermocouple measurements.

Word Families: **coincidence** *n.;* **coincidently** *adv.*

SENTENCE COMPLETION

Choose one of the new words to complete each sentence below. Make changes if necessary.

| protocol | menthol | alcohol | parasol | cholesterol |
| provident | diffident | evident | incident | coincident |

1. They are determining the serum-protein and _____ levels.

2. He felt a little _____ about asking concerning her success.

3. The truth was by no means _____ when Galileo first suggested it.

4. _____ is often a very potent trigger for cluster headache, as well.

5. We must observe the correct _____ in business.

6. The police said that the attack was an isolated _____.

7. Mary has been _____ ever since she was a little girl.

8. The _____ in the toothpaste gives a cooling sensation.

9. The results of model experiments are well _____ with those of finite element method.

10. All kinds of umbrellas include stick, folder, beach, golf and _____.

DEFINITION MATCHING

Choose one of the new words to match each definition below.

| protocol | menthol | alcohol | parasol | cholesterol |
| provident | diffident | evident | incident | coincident |

11. in agreement   _____

12. umbrella-like sunshade   _____

13. fatty substance found in animal tissue   _____

14. event involving violence   _____

15. easy to see, notice, or understand   _____

16. rules of behavior for formal occasions   _____

17. thrifty; showing foresight   _____

18. shy   _____

19. a substance that smells and tastes like mint   _____

20. intoxicating drinks generally   _____

WRITING SENTENCES

Use each new word in the box to write an original sentence.

protocol	menthol	alcohol	parasol	cholesterol
provident	diffident	evident	incident	coincident

21. _____
22. _____
23. _____
24. _____
25. _____
26. _____
27. _____
28. _____
29. _____
30. _____

UNIT 32

MEMORY TIPS:

Word building with Roots, Prefixes, and Suffixes:

ad	to; as *adjoin*
dis	apart, not; as *disjoin*
ex	out of, from; as *exile*
ile	capable of being; as *puerile, agile, docile, futile*

NEW WORDS

puerile	agile	docile	exile	futile
purloin	adjoin	conjoin	disjoin	rejoin

1. **PUERILE** ['pjʊrəl] *adj.* silly and childish   **rhyming sound –ile**

    His **puerile** pranks sometimes offended his more mature friends.
    Word Families: **puerility** *n.;* **puerilely** *adv.*

2. **agile** ['æˌdʒəl] *adj.* able to move quickly and easily

    His intellect and mental **agility** have never been in doubt.
    Word Families: **agility** *n;* **agilely** *adv.*

3. **docile** ['dɒsɪl] *adj.* (of a person or animal) easily controlled

    The soldiers were grateful and **docile**, made almost childlike by their wounds.

Word Families: **docility** *n.;* **docilely** *adv.*

4. **futile** ['fjut(ə)l] *adj.* unsuccessful, or useless

Without microscopes and other modern equipment, attempts to teach science were **futile**.

Word Families: **futility** *n.;* **futilely** *adv.*

5. **revile** [rɪ'vaɪl] *v.* to hate and criticize someone or something very much

Meanwhile, the Bosnian Muslims **revile** them (peacekeepers) for standing by when women and children are shot.

Word Families: **revilement** *n.;* **reviler** *n.*

6. **PURLOIN** [pər'lɔɪn] *v.* to steal something secretly   **rhyming sound -oin**

Everyone is issued a user name and a password so secret that it has to be hidden in a "safe place" lest someone **purloins** it.

7. **adjoin** [ə'dʒɔɪn] *v.* to be next to

Canada and Mexico **adjoin** the United States of America.

Word Families: **adjoining** *adj.*

8. **conjoin** [kən'dʒɔɪn] *v.* to join two or more things, or become joined

All this will occur because on September 3, Saturn will **conjoin** the Sun.

9. **disjoin** [dɪs'dʒɔɪn] *v.* to disconnect parts, things, or ideas

After you **disjoin** the domain, shut down the client computer before you reconnect it to the new domain.

10. **rejoin** [ˌri'dʒɔɪn] *v.* to join again

However, by its full compliance, Iraq will gain the opportunity to **rejoin** the international community.

SENTENCE COMPLETION

Choose one of the new words to complete each sentence below. Make changes if necessary.

puerile	agile	docile	exile	futile
purloin	adjoin	conjoin	disjoin	rejoin

1. Circus monkeys are trained to be very _____ and obedient.

2. We waited in an _____ office.

3. Thou shall not _____ the gods, nor curse the ruler of you people.

4. He said that he never heard anything so _____ before.

5. The next big day to watch will be Sunday, March 7, when Mercury will _____ Jupiter.

6. Some countries _____ American technology as it comes off the drawing boards with the help of their governments.

7. Just as physical exercise is essential for a strong body, mental exercise is equally essential for a sharp and _____ mind.

8. Henry has apologized for his bad behavior and should be allowed to _____ the group with a clean sheet.

9. It can lift rate of zinc reclamation, _____ the lead and zinc.

10. It is always _____ to try to hold back the progress of history.

DEFINITION MATCHING

Choose one of the new words to match each definition below.

puerile	agile	docile	exile	futile
purloin	adjoin	conjoin	disjoin	rejoin

11. to be next to _____

12. to join again _____

13. to join two or more things, or become joined _____

14. to disconnect parts, things, or ideas _____

15. to steal something secretly _____

16. silly and childish _____

17. to hate and criticize someone or something _____

18. (of a person or animal) easily controlled _____

19. unsuccessful, or useless _____

20. able to move quickly and easily _____

WRITING SENTENCES

Use each new word in the box to write an original sentence.

puerile	agile	docile	exile	futile
purloin	adjoin	conjoin	disjoin	rejoin

21. _____

22. _____

23. _____

24. _____

25. _____

26. _____

27. _____

28. _____

29. _____

30. _____

UNIT 33

MEMORY TIPS:

Word building with Roots, Prefixes, and Suffixes:

ify	make, cause; as *putrefy, classify, justify, qualify, sanctify*
inter	between, among; as *interview*
pre	before; as *preview*
re	back, again; as *review*
sanct	holy; as *sanctify*

NEW WORDS

purview	preview	review	worldview	interview
putrefy	classify	justify	qualify	sanctify

1. PURVIEW ['pɜrvju] *n.* scope or range of activity or outlook   **rhyming sound –iew**

These are questions that lie outside the **purview** of our inquiry.

2. preview ['pri,vju] *n.* advance showing of a film or exhibition; *v.* to provide a description of something that will happen in the future

You will be able to see a **preview** of the image that you upload.

Word Families: **previews** *n. pl.*

3. review [rɪ'vju] *n.* critical assessment of a book, film, etc.; *v.* to examine

Officials said the investigation does not amount to a full safety **review**.

Word Families: **reviewal** *n.;* **reviewable** *adj.*

4. worldview ['wɜːldvjuː] *n.* the way one sees and understands the world events

Worldview is total knowledge and evaluation of human to the whole world.

5. interview ['ɪntərˌvju] *adj.* questioning of someone or a famous person; discussion between a job-seeker and employer; *v.* to conduct an interview with

There'll be an **interview** with Mr. Brown after the news.

Word Families: **interviewee** *n.;* **interviewer** *n.*

6. PUTREFY ['pjutrɪˌfaɪ] *v.* to decay   rhyming sound –fy, -ify

Incomplete pre-digestion process causes partially digested proteins to **putrefy** in the intestines forming toxic substances.

7. classify ['klæsəˌfaɪ] *v.* to divide into groups with similar characteristics; to declare (information) to be officially secret

Rocks can be **classified** according to their mode of origin.

Word Families: **classification** *n.;* **classifiable** *adj.*

8. justify ['dʒʌstɪˌfaɪ] *v.* to prove right or reasonable

Several reasons were put forward to **justify** the imposition of censorship.

Word Families: **justification** *n.;* **justifier** *n.;* **justificatory** *adj.*

9. qualify ['kwɑləˌfaɪ] *v.* to provide or be provided with the abilities for a task

To **qualify** for maternity leave, you must have worked for the same employer for at least two years.

Word Families: **qualification** *n;* **qualifier** *n.;* **qualified** *adj.*

10. sanctify ['sæŋktəˌfaɪ] *v.* to make someone or something holy

I believe that it is one of the special achievements of Grace to **sanctify** the whole of life, riches included.

Word Families: **sanctification** *n.;* **sanctifier** *n.;* **sanctifiable** *adj.*

SENTENCE COMPLETION

Choose one of the new words to complete each sentence below. Make changes if necessary.

| purview | preview | review | worldview | interview |
| putrefy | classify | justify | qualify | sanctify |

1. Am I going to allow bitterness to poison and _____ my soul, or am I going to invite God to empower me to let the anger go?

2. The _____ is uncritical of the violence in the film.

3. The police immediately _____ the man's death as a suicide.

4. They attended a sneak _____ of the winter fashion collection.

5. My intellect was on call to expand its _____ and comprehend.

6. They found it hard to _____ their son's lowering his colors.

7. Mental imagery belongs to the _____ of philosophy and cognitive psychology.

8. She is trying to make amends for her marriage not being _____.

9. Our team _____ for the final by beating Vancouver Canucks on Tuesday.

10. The police _____ the driver, but had no evidence to go on.

DEFINITION MATCHING

Choose one of the new words to match each definition below.

| purview | preview | review | worldview | interview |
| putrefy | classify | justify | qualify | sanctify |

11. to declare (information) to be officially secret   _____

12. to provide or be provided with the abilities for   _____

13. the way one sees and understands world events _____

14. to make someone or something holy _____

15. to prove right or reasonable _____

16. advance showing of a film or exhibition _____

17. to decay _____

18. scope or range of activity or outlook _____

19. critical assessment of a book, film, etc. _____

20. questioning of someone or a famous person _____

WRITING SENTENCES

Use each new word in the box to write an original sentence.

purview	preview	review	worldview	interview
putrefy	classify	justify	qualify	sanctify

21. _____
22. _____
23. _____
24. _____
25. _____
26. _____
27. _____
28. _____
29. _____
30. _____

UNIT 34

MEMORY TIPS:

Word building with Roots, Prefixes, and Suffixes:

ac, as	to; as *acquire, aspire*
con	together; as *conspire*
mar	sea; as *marine*

NEW WORDS

quagmire	acquire	aspire	conspire	respire
quarantine	chlorine	cuisine	marine	pristine

1. QUAGMIRE ['kwæg,maɪr] *n.* soft wet area of land   **rhyming sound –ire**

He who tries to conceal his fault for fear of criticism will sink deeper and deeper in the **quagmire** of errors.

Word Families: **quagmires** *n. pl.*

2. acquire [əˈkwaɪr] *v.* to gain; to get

Should Iraq **acquire** fissile material, it would be able to build a nuclear weapon within a year.

Word Families: **acquisition** *n.;* **acquiree** *n.;* **acquirer** *n.;* **acquirable** *adj.*

3. aspire [əˈspaɪr] *n.* to want to achieve something or to be successful

Literally, he lived only to **aspire** after what was good and great, certainly.

Word Families: **aspiration** *n.*

4. **conspire**   [kən'spaɪr] *v.* to plan a crime (something bad) together in secret

The oil companies **conspire** every year to increase the price of oil.

Word Families: **conspiracy** *n.;* **conspirator** *n.;* **conspiratorial** *adj.*

5. **respire**   [rɪ'spaɪr] *v.* to breathe

He also discovered that plants **respire** in the same way as animals, taking up oxygen and giving out carbon dioxide.

Word Families: **respiration** *n.;* **respiratory** *adj.*

6. **QUARANTINE** ['kwɔrən,tin] *n.* a period of enforced seclusion to prevent contagion
rhyming sound -ine

The health officials placed the ship's crew in **quarantine**.

7. **chlorine**   ['klɔrin] *n.* a gas with a strong smell used to kill bacteria in the pool

Her eyes were red and sore because of all the **chlorine** in the pool.

8. **cuisine**   [kwɪ'zin] *n.* style of cooking

This village has its own traditional dress, **cuisine**, folklore and handicrafts.

Word Families: **cuisine** *n.pl.*

9. **marine**   [mə'rin] *adj.* living in or happening in the ocean; *n.* a soldier in the marine corps.

He was one of eighteen researchers who wrote the **Marine** Policy paper.

10. **pristine**   ['prɪ,stin] *adj.* clean, new, and unused

The secret behind the **pristine** complexion of these exotic women was Pearl Powder.

SENTENCE COMPLETION

Choose one of the new words to complete each sentence below. Make changes if necessary.

quagmire	acquire	aspire	conspire	respire
quarantine	chlorine	cuisine	marine	pristine

1. General Motors _____ a 50% stake in Saab for about $400 million.

2. The dog was kept in _____ for six months.

3. The hotel has a large dining room serving superb local _____.

4. They _____ to be gentlemen, though they fell far short of the ideal.

5. If you think your water has a strong taste of _____, try boiling it.

6. They tried artificial _____ but it was of no avail.

7. The heavy rain had turned the pitch into a _____.

8. Those who plot and _____ will certainly come to no good end.

9. New Zealand is renowned for the _____, natural beauty of its environment beyond comparison.

10. Aides to the president say Mr. Bush has protected more of the _____ environment than any of his predecessors.

DEFINITION MATCHING

Choose one of the new words to match each definition below.

quagmire	acquire	aspire	conspire	respire
quarantine	chlorine	cuisine	marine	pristine

11. to breathe   _____

12. living in or happening in the ocean   _____

13. soft wet area of land   _____

14. time for enforced seclusion to prevent contagion _____

15. clean, new, and unused _____

16. to want to achieve something or to be successful _____

17. style of cooking _____

18. a gas with a strong smell used to kill bacteria _____

19. to gain; to get _____

20. to plan a crime (bad things) together in secret _____

WRITING SENTENCES

Use each new word in the box to write an original sentence.

quagmire	acquire	aspire	conspire	respire
quarantine	chlorine	cuisine	marine	pristine

21. _____
22. _____
23. _____
24. _____
25. _____
26. _____
27. _____
28. _____
29. _____
30. _____

UNIT 35

MEMORY TIPS:

Word building with Roots, Prefixes, and Suffixes:

chron	time; as *chronological*
ence	state of; as *sequence, diligence, indulgence, quintessence, intelligence*
il	not; as *illogical*
in	into, in, on; as *indulgence*

NEW WORDS

quintessence	sequence	diligence	indulgence	intelligence
quizzical	radical	illogical	sabbatical	chronological

1. **QUINTESSENCE** [kwɪnˈtes(ə)ns] *n.* most perfect representation of quality or state

    rhyming sound –ence

    The development and evolution of liberalism show the **quintessence** of the two political traditions from beginning to end.

    Word Families: **quintessential** *adj.*

2. **sequence** [ˈsikwəns] *n.* the successive order of two or more things

    The book is more satisfying if you read each chapter in **sequence**.

3. **diligence** [ˈdɪlɪdʒəns] *n.* care and perseverance

Genius is nothing but wit and **diligence**.

Word Families: **diligent** *adj.;* **diligently** *adj.*

4. **indulgence** [ɪnˈdʌldʒəns] *n.* act of doing something that is not good for you

The woman seldom allows herself any moment of **indulgence** in self-pity.

Word Families: **indulgences** *n. pl.*

5. **intelligence** [ɪnˈtelɪdʒəns] *n.* quality of being intelligent; secret government or military information

She used her good looks to compensate her lack of **intelligence**.

Families: **intelligent** *adj.*

6. **QUIZZICAL** [ˈkwɪzɪkəl] *adj.* questioning and mocking   **rhyming sound -ical**

His face wore a somewhat **quizzical**, almost impertinent air.

Word Families: **quizzicality** *n.;* **quizzically** *adv.*

7. **radical** [ˈrædɪk(ə)l] *adj.* advocating drastic reform of existing institutions; *n.* an extreme liberal in politics

The county now needs stability instead of **radical** changes in its policies.

Word Families: **radicalism** *n.;* **radically** *adv.*

8. **illogical** [ɪˈlɑdʒɪk(ə)l] *adj.* not based on clear facts, reasons, or principles

There are some people who will use any kind of argument, no matter how **illogical**, so long as they can score off an opponent.

Word Families: **illogicality** *n.;* **illogically** *adv.*

9. **sabbatical** [səˈbætɪk(ə)l] *adj., n.* (denoting) leave for study, rest, or travel

Dr. Samuel Johnson is on **sabbatical** in Europe this year.

Word Families: **sabbaticals** *n.pl.*

10. **chronological** [ˌkrɑnəˈlɑdʒɪk(ə)l] *adj.* arranged or listed in the order of occurrence

The paintings are exhibited in **chronological** sequence.

Word Families: **chronologically** *adv.*

SENTENCE COMPLETION

Choose one of the new words to complete each sentence below. Make changes if necessary.

| quintessence | sequence | diligence | indulgence | intelligence |
| quizzical | radical | illogical | sabbatical | chronological |

1. The police are pursuing their inquiries with great _____.
2. He had a _____ expression on his face when he got in.
3. It is clearly _____ to maintain such a proposition.
4. He was the _____ of all that Eva most deeply loathed.
5. There was some sort of _____ psychiatric treatment involved.
6. Jenny Jones spent her _____ writing a novel.
7. The project is nothing less than mapping every gene _____ in the human body.
8. The purpose of _____ is to provide information on how the enemy can be beaten.
9. The car is one of my few _____.
10. The items are arranged in _____ order, with the most recent at the top.

DEFINITION MATCHING

Choose one of the new words to match each definition below.

| quintessence | sequence | diligence | indulgence | intelligence |
| quizzical | radical | illogical | sabbatical | chronological |

11. an extreme liberal in politics   _____

12. (denoting) leave for study, rest, or travel _____

13. the successive order of two or more things _____

14. arranged or listed in the order of occurrence _____

15. not based on clear facts, reasons, or principles _____

16. act of doing something that is not good for you _____

17. quality of being intelligent _____

18. most perfect of quality or state _____

19. questioning and mocking _____

20. care and perseverance _____

WRITING SENTENCES

Use each new word in the box to write an original sentence.

quintessence	sequence	diligence	indulgence	intelligence
quizzical	radical	illogical	sabbatical	chronological

21. _____
22. _____
23. _____
24. _____
25. _____
26. _____
27. _____
28. _____
29. _____
30. _____

ANSWER KEY

UNIT 1

SENTENCE COMPLETION

1. inauspicious 2. rotund 3. laborious 4. jocund 5. rubicund 6. pernicious 7. moribund 8. refund 9. prejudicious 10. avaricious

DEFINITION MATCHING

11. rotund 12. laborious 13. rubicund 14. prejudicious 15. refund 16. pernicious 17. avaricious 18. moribund 19. inauspicious 20. jocund

WRITING SENTENCES

Answers will vary based on students' personal experiences.

UNIT 2

SENTENCE COMPLETION

1. advocates 2. lambent 3. lacerated 4. imminent 5. precipitate 6. nascent 7. intimidate 8. pertinent 9. consolidated 10. penitent

DEFINITION MATCHING

11. precipitate 12. pertinent 13. consolidate 14. penitent 15. intimidate 16. lacerate 17. imminent 18. lambent 19. nascent 20. advocate

WRITING SENTENCES

Answers will vary based on students' personal experiences.

UNIT 3

SENTENCE COMPLETION

1. largess 2. lampoon 3. digress 4. duress 5. monsoon 6. lagoon 7. obsess 8. platoon 9. tycoon 10. transgress

DEFINITION MATCHING

11. digress 12. obsess 13. duress 14. monsoon 15. transgress 16. tycoon 17. largess 18. lagoon 19. platoon 20. lampoon

WRITING SENTENCES

Answers will vary based on students' personal experiences.

UNIT 4

SENTENCE COMPLETION

1. profusion 2. precision 3. conducive 4. legion 5. abortive 6. cumulatively 7. introversion 8. lucrative 9. fusions 10. diminutive

DEFINITION MATCHING

11. abortive 12. lucrative 13. fusion 14. diminutive 15. precision 16. cumulative 17. introversion 18. legion 19. conducive 20. profusion

WRITING SENTENCES

Answers will vary based on students' personal experiences.

UNIT 5

SENTENCE COMPLETION

1. rid 2. dull 3. acrid 4. lurid 5. lull 6. forbid 7. gull 8. skull 9. null 10. rigid

DEFINITION MATCHING

11. lurid 12. null 13. acrid 14. forbid 15. rigid 16. lull 17. skull 18. gull 19. rid 20. dull

WRITING SENTENCES

Answers will vary based on students' personal experiences.

UNIT 6

SENTENCE COMPLETION

1. addiction 2. jurisdiction 3. convictions 4. malediction 5. resign 6. consign 7. malign 8. friction 9. assign 10. align

DEFINITION MATCHING

11. align 12. addiction 13. jurisdiction 14. consign 15. friction 16. conviction 17. resign 18. malign 19. assign 20. malediction

WRITING SENTENCES

Answers will vary based on students' personal experiences.

UNIT 7

SENTENCE COMPLETION

1. morality 2. mercenary 3. fatality 4. materiality 5. centenary 6. formality 7. planetary 8. mortuary 9. brutality 10. adversary

DEFINITION MATCHING

11. mortuary 12. morality 13. planetary 14. fatality 15. centenary 16. materiality 17. mercenary 18. adversary 19. brutality 20. formality

WRITING SENTENCES

Answers will vary based on students' personal experiences.

UNIT 8

SENTENCE COMPLETION

1. oscillate 2. mitigate 3. mollify 4. propagate 5. certify 6. innate 7. rectify 8. ossify 9. vilification 10. emulate

DEFINITION MATCHING

11. vilify 12. rectify 13. ossify 14. innate 15. certify 16. oscillate 17. emulate 18. propagate 19. mollify 20. mitigate

WRITING SENTENCES

Answers will vary based on students' personal experiences.

UNIT 9

SENTENCE COMPLETION

1. penchant 2. mordant 3. morose 4. recalcitrant 5. verbose 6. foreclose 7. petulant 8. dispose 9. compose 10. rampant

DEFINITION MATCHING

11. petulant 12. verbose 13. foreclose 14. recalcitrant 15. dispose 16. mordant 17. morose 18. compose 19. penchant 20. rampant

WRITING SENTENCES

Answers will vary based on students' personal experiences.

UNIT 10

SENTENCE COMPLETION

1. insane 2. humane 3. extent 4. mundane 5. aliment 6. hurricane 7. consented 8. regiment 9. profaned 10. munificent

DEFINITION MATCHING

11. regiment 12. consent 13. aliment 14. profane 15. extent 16. mundane 17. hurricane 18. humane 19. munificent 20. insane

WRITING SENTENCES

Answers will vary based on students' personal experiences.

UNIT 11

SENTENCE COMPLETION

1. precarious 2. tererarious 3. multifarious 4. vicarious 5. mimesis 6. nefarious 7. nemesis 8. thesis 9. telekinesis 10. exegesis

DEFINITION MATCHING

11. telekinesis 12. multifarious 13. precarious 14. exegesis 15. mimesis 16. nefarious 17. thesis 18. tererarious 19. nemesis 20. vicarious

WRITING SENTENCES

Answers will vary based on students' personal experiences.

UNIT 12

SENTENCE COMPLETION

1. atmospheric 2. troglodyte 3. esoteric 4. neoteric 5. neophyte 6. byte 7. acolyte 8. proselytes 9. generic 10. numeric

DEFINITION MATCHING

11. troglodyte 12. esoteric 13. acolyte 14. neoteric 15. neophyte 16. atmospheric 17. numeric 18. byte 19. generic 20. proselyte

WRITING SENTENCES

Answers will vary based on students' personal experiences.

UNIT 13

SENTENCE COMPLETION

1. fettle 2. nettle 3. discard 4. niggard 5. retard 6. settled 7. safeguards 8. mettle 9. bard 10. unsettle

DEFINITION MATCHING

11. retard 12. settle 13. safeguard 14. unsettle 15. discard 16. nettle 17. bard 18. niggard 19. mettle 20. fettle

WRITING SENTENCES

Answers will vary based on students' personal experiences.

UNIT 14

SENTENCE COMPLETION

1. nutritious 2. precious 3. obnoxious 4. noxious 5. signatory 6. purgatory 7. nugatory 8. defamatory 9. ostentatious 10. mandatory

DEFINITION MATCHING

11. obnoxious 12. purgatory 13. nutritious 14. signatory 15. mandatory 16. noxious 17. defamatory 18. ostentatious 19. nugatory 20. precious

WRITING SENTENCES

Answers will vary based on students' personal experiences.

UNIT 15

SENTENCE COMPLETION

1. renaissance 2. nuance 3. castigate 4. obeisance 5. articulate 6. enhance 7. inveterate 8. askance 9. obfuscate 10. deprecate

DEFINITION MATCHING

11. castigate 12. deprecate 13. enhance 14. articulate 15. inveterate 16. obeisance 17. obfuscate 18. nuance 19. renaissance 20. askance

WRITING SENTENCES

Answers will vary based on students' personal experiences.

UNIT 16

SENTENCE COMPLETION

1. extrapolate 2. deludes 3. obtrude 4. enunciate 5. aptitudes 6. rectitude 7. exculpated 8. lassitude 9. objurgate 10. facilitate

DEFINITION MATCHING

11. aptitude 12. rectitude 13. lassitude 14. extrapolate 15. delude 16. objurgate 17. facilitate 18. exculpate 19. obtrude 20. enunciate

WRITING SENTENCES

Answers will vary based on students' personal experiences.

UNIT 17

SENTENCE COMPLETION

1. fractious 2. hierarchy 3. oligarchy 4. odious 5. patriarchy 6. anarchy 7. facetious 8. monarchy 9. disputatious 10. fortuitous

DEFINITION MATCHING

11. anarchy 12. hierarchy 13. facetious 14. fortuitous 15. patriarchy 16. odious 17. oligarchy 18. monarchy 19. fractious 20. disputatious

WRITING SENTENCES

Answers will vary based on students' personal experiences.

UNIT 18

SENTENCE COMPLETION

1. adolescent 2. fervent 3. captious 4. horrendous 5. opalescence 6. putrescent 7. lecherous 8. opprobrious 9. ferment 10. mellifluous

DEFINITION MATCHING

11. lecherous 12. mellifluous 13. ferment 14. horrendous 15. opprobrious 16. opalescent 17. captious 18. fervent 19. adolescent 20. putrescent

WRITING SENTENCES

Answers will vary based on students' personal experiences.

UNIT 19

SENTENCE COMPLETION

1. clone 2. inculcate 3. condone 4. immaculately 5. cyclone 6. instigate 7. ozone 8. originate 9. silicone 10. litigate

DEFINITION MATCHING

11. immaculate 12. cyclone 13. inculcate 14. silicone 15. condone 16. originate 17. clone 18. litigate 19. ozone 20. instigate

WRITING SENTENCES

Answers will vary based on students' personal experiences.

UNIT 20

SENTENCE COMPLETION

1. tractable 2. Equinox 3. palpable 4. smallpox 5. orthodox 6. jukebox 7. immutable 8. irreparable 9. paradox 10. viable

DEFINITION MATCHING

11. equinox 12. orthodox 13. tractable 14. smallpox 15. jukebox 16. palpable 17. paradox 18. irreparable 19. viable 20. immutable

WRITING SENTENCES

Answers will vary based on students' personal experiences.

UNIT 21

SENTENCE COMPLETION

1. disparity 2. amorphous 3. brevity 4. alacrity 5. arduous 6. depravity 7. parity

8. anonymous 9. ambiguous 10. parsimonious

DEFINITION MATCHING

11. ambiguous 12. anonymous 13. arduous 14. alacrity 15. amorphous 16. parity 17. parsimonious 18. depravity 19. brevity 20. disparity

WRITING SENTENCES

Answers will vary based on students' personal experiences.

UNIT 22

SENTENCE COMPLETION

1. impunity 2. paucity 3. jury 4. fury 5. humility 6. penury 7. probity 8. perjury 9. frugality 10. Mercury

DEFINITION MATCHING

11. impunity 12. mercury 13. probity 14. jury 15. perjury 16. penury 17. paucity 18. fury 19. frugality 20. humility

WRITING SENTENCES

Answers will vary based on students' personal experiences.

UNIT 23

SENTENCE COMPLETION

1. abnegation 2. implication 3. allegory 4. perdition 5. peremptory 6. adulation 7. dilatory 8. aspersion 9. perfunctory 10. Inventory

DEFINITION MATCHING

11. implication 12. inventory 13. allegory 14. perfunctory 15. perdition 16. peremptory 17. dilatory 18. abnegation 19. adulation 20. aspersion

WRITING SENTENCES

Answers will vary based on students' personal experiences.

UNIT 24

SENTENCE COMPLETION

1. momentous 2. vociferous 3. tenuous 4. peruse 5. perfidious 6. ominously 7. fuse 8. abused 9. interfusion 10. muse

DEFINITION MATCHING

11. muse 12. interfuse 13. perfidious 14. abuse 15. fuse 16. tenuous 17. vociferous 18. peruse 19. ominous 20. momentous

WRITING SENTENCES

Answers will vary based on students' personal experiences.

UNIT 25

SENTENCE COMPLETION

1. evasiveness 2. dissuasive 3. persuasive 4. pervasive 5. intuition 6. coalition 7. rendition 8. acquisition 9. abrasive 10. petition

DEFINITION MATCHING

11. petition 12. rendition 13. abrasive 14. acquisition 15. intuition 16. persuasive 17. dissuasive 18. coalition 19. evasive 20. pervasive

WRITING SENTENCES

UNIT 26

SENTENCE COMPLETION

1. systemic 2. endemic 3. epistemic 4. polemic 5. portend 6. blend 7. epidemic 8. reprehended 9. apprehend 10. amend

DEFINITION MATCHING

11. apprehend 12. reprehend 13. polemic 14. amend 15. blend 16. endemic 17. portend 18. epidemic 19. epistemic 20. systemic

WRITING SENTENCES

Answers will vary based on students' personal experiences.

UNIT 27

SENTENCE COMPLETION

1. spaciousness 2. specious 3. inception 4. atrocious 5. concept 6. intercepted 7. precept 8. inept 9. ferocious 10. precocious

DEFINITION MATCHING

11. precocious 12. specious 13. precept 14. intercept 15. ferocious 16. concept 17. atrocious 18. spacious 19. incept 20. inept

WRITING SENTENCES

Answers will vary based on students' personal experiences.

UNIT 28

SENTENCE COMPLETION

1. profligate 2. repudiate 3. elaborate 4. preponderate 5. prerogative 6. prate 7. preservative 8. derivative 9. figurative 10. correlative

DEFINITION MATCHING

11. profligate 12. prerogative 13. preponderate 14. preservative 15. figurative 16. prate 17. derivative 18. repudiate 19. correlative 20. elaborate

WRITING SENTENCES

Answers will vary based on students' personal experiences.

UNIT 29

SENTENCE COMPLETION

1. scoliosis 2. prolific 3. prognosis 4. specific 5. horrific 6. Diagnosis 7. terrific 8. colorific 9. hypnosis 10. Tuberculosis

DEFINITION MATCHING

11. tuberculosis 12. horrific 13. colorific 14. scoliosis 15. terrific 16. hypnosis 17. specific 18. diagnosis 19. prolific 20. prognosis

WRITING SENTENCES

Answers will vary based on students' personal experiences.

UNIT 30

SENTENCE COMPLETION

1. relegate 2. deviated 3. eradication 4. prognosticate 5. differentiate 6. initiated 7. implicate 8. propitiate 9. mediate 10. reiterate

DEFINITION MATCHING

11. eradicate 12. differentiate 13. propitiate 14. mediate 15. initiate 16. prognosticate 17. reiterate 18. deviate 19. implicate 20. relegate

WRITING SENTENCES

Answers will vary based on students' personal experiences.

UNIT 31

SENTENCE COMPLETION

1. cholesterol 2. diffident 3. evident 4. alcohol 5. protocol 6. incident 7. provident 8. menthol 9. coincident 10. parasol

DEFINITION MATCHING

11. coincident 12. parasol 13. cholesterol 14. incident 15. evident 16. protocol 17. provident 18. diffident 19. menthol 20. alcohol

WRITING SENTENCES

Answers will vary based on students' personal experiences.

UNIT 32

SENTENCE COMPLETION

1. docile 2. adjoining 3. revile 4. puerile 5. conjoin 6. purloin 7. agile 8. rejoin 9. disjoin 10. futile

DEFINITION MATCHING

11. adjoining 12. rejoin 13. conjoin 14. disjoin 15. purloin 16. puerile 17. revile 18. docile 19. futile 20. agile

WRITING SENTENCES

Answers will vary based on students' personal experiences.

UNIT 33

SENTENCE COMPLETION

1. putrefy 2. review 3. classified 4. preview 5. worldview 6. justify 7. purview 8. sanctified 9. qualified 10. interviewed

DEFINITION MATCHING

11. classify 12. qualify 13. worldview 14. sanctify 15. justify 16. preview 17. putrefy 18. purview 19. review 20. interview

WRITING SENTENCES

Answers will vary based on students' personal experiences.

UNIT 34

SENTENCE COMPLETION

1. acquired 2. quarantine 3. cuisine 4. aspired 5. chlorine 6. respiration 7. quagmire 8. conspire 9. pristine 10. marine

DEFINITION MATCHING

11. respire 12. marine 13. quagmire 14.

quarantine 15. pristine 16. aspire 17. cuisine 18. chlorine 19. acquire 20. conspire

WRITING SENTENCES

Answers will vary based on students' personal experiences.

UNIT 35

SENTENCE COMPLETION

1. diligence 2. quizzical 3. illogical 4. quintessence 5. radical 6. sabbatical 7. sequence 8. intelligence 9. indulgences 10. chronological

DEFINITION MATCHING

11. radical 12. sabbatical 13. sequence 14. chronological 15. illogical 16. indulgence 17. intelligence 18. quintessence 19. quizzical 20. diligence

WRITING SENTENCES

Answers will vary based on students' personal experiences.

WORD INDEX

This index lists 350 absolutely essential SAT key words appeared in this book. You may use the list as a dictionary to find out the definitions, samples sentences, and the uses of each word to boost your retention.

A

Abnegation 100

Abortive 24

Abrasive 108

Abuse 104

Acolyte 56

Acquisition 108

Acrid 28

Addiction 32

Adjoin 136

Adolescent 80

Adulation 100

Adversary 36

Advocate 16

Agile 136

Alacrity 92

Alcohol 132

Align 32

Aliment 48

Allegory 100

Ambiguous 92

Amend 112

Amorphous 92

Anarchy 76

Anonymous 92

Apprehend 112

Aptitude 72

Acquire 144

Arduous 92

Articulate 68

Askance 68

Aspersion 100

Aspire 144

Assign 32

Atmospheric 56

Atrocious 116

Avaricious 12

B

Bard 60

Blend 112

Brevity 92

Brutality 36

Byte 56

C

Captious 80

Castigate 68

Centenary 36

Certify 40

Chlorine 144

Cholesterol 132

Chronological 148

Classify 140

Clone 84

Coalition 108

Coincident 132

Colorific 124

Compose 44

Concept 116

Condone 84

Conducive 24

Conjoin 136

Consent 48

Consign 32

Consolidate 16

Conspire 144

Conviction 32

Correlative 120

Cuisine 144

Cumulative 24

Cyclone 84

D

Defamatory 64

Delude 72

Depravity 92

Deprecate 68

Derivative 120

Deviate 128

Diagnosis 124

Differentiate 128

Diffident 132

Digress 20

Dilatory 100

Diligence 148

Diminutive 24

Discard 60

Disjoin 136

Disparity 92

Dispose 44

Disputatious 76

Dissuasive 108

Docile 136

Dull 28

Duress 20

E

Elaborate 120

Emulate 40

Enunciate 72

Endemic 112

Enhance 68

Epidemic 112

Epistemic 112

Equinox 88

Eradicate 128

Esoteric 56

Evasive 108

Evident 132

Exculpate 72

Exegesis 52

Exile 136

Extent 48

Extrapolate 72

F

Facetious 76

Facilitate 72

Factious 76

Fatality 36

Ferment 80

Ferocious 116

Fervent 80

Fettle 60

Figurative 120

Forbid 28

Foreclose 44

Formality 36

Fortuitous 76

Friction 32

Frugality 96

Fury 96

Fuse 104

Fusion 24

Futile 136

G

Generic 56

Gull 28

H

Hierarchy 76

Horrendous 80

Horrific 124

Humane 48

Humility 96

Hurricane 48

Hypnosis 124

I

Illogical 148

Immaculate 84

Imminent 16

Immutable 88

Implicate 128

Implication 100

Impunity 96

Inauspicious 12

Incept 116

Incident 132

Inculcate 84

Indulgence 148

Inept 116

Initiate 128

Innate 40

Insane 48

Instigate 84

Intelligence 148

Intercept 116

Interfuse 104

Interview 140

Intimidate 16

Introversion 24

Intuition 108

Inventory 100

Inveterate 68

Irreparable 88

J

Jocund 12

Jukebox 88

Jurisdiction 32

Jury 96

Justify 140

L

Laborious 12

Lacerate 16

Lambent 16

Lagoon 20

Lampoon 20

Largess 20

Lassitude 72

Lecherous 80

Legion 24

Litigate 84

Lucrative 24

Lull 28

Lurid 28

M

Malediction 32

Malign 32

Mandatory 64

Marine 144

Materiality 36

Mediate 128

Mellifluous 80

Mimesis 52

Menthol 132

Mercenary 36

Mercury 96

Mettle 60

Mitigate 40

Mollify 40

Momentous 104

Monarchy 76

Monsoon 20

Morality 36

Mordant 44

Moribund 12

Morose 44

Mortuary 36

Multifarious 52

Mundane 48

Munificent 48

Muse 104

N

Nascent 16

Nefarious 52

Nemesis 52

Neophyte 56

Neoteric 56

Nettle 60

Niggard 60

Noxious 64

Nuance 68

Nugatory 64

Null 28

Numeric 56

Nutritious 64

O

Obeisance 68

Obfuscate 68

Objurgate 72

Obsess 20

Obtrude 72

Odious 76

Oligarchy 76

Ominous 104

Opalescent 80

Opprobrious 80

Originate 84

Orthodox 88

Oscillate 40

Ossify 40

Ostentatious 64

Ozone 83

P

Palpable 88

Paradox 88

Parasol 132

Parity 92

Parsimonious 92

Patriarchy 76

Paucity 96

Penchant 44

Penitent 16

Penury 96

Perdition 100

Peremptory 100

Perfidious 104

Perfunctory 100

Perjury 96

Pernicious 12

Persuasive 108

Pertinent 16

Peruse 104

Pervasive 108

Petition 108

Petulant 44

Planetary 36

Platoon 20

Polemic 112

Portend 112

Prate 120

Precarious 52

Precept 116

Precious 64

Precipitate 16

Precision 24

Precocious 116

Prejudicious 12

Preponderate 120

Prerogative 120

Preservative 120

Preview 140

Pristine 144

Probity 96

Profane 48

Profligate 120

Profusion 24

Prognosis 124

Prognosticate 128

Prolific 124

Propagate 40

Propitiate 128

Proselyte 56

Protocol 132

Provident 132

Puerile 136

Purgatory 64

Purloin 136

Purview 140

Putrefy 140

Putrescent 80

Q

Quagmire 144

Qualify 140

Quarantine 144

Quintessence 148

Quizzical 148

R

Radical 148

Rampant 44

Recalcitrant 44

Rectify 40

Rectitude 72

Refund 12

Regiment 48

Reiterate 128

Rejoin 136

Relegate 128

Renaissance 68

Rendition 108

Reprehend 112

Repudiate 120

Resign 32

Respire 144

Retard 60

Review 140

Rid 28

Rigid 28

Rotund 12

Rubicund 12

S

Sabbatical 148

Safeguard 60

Sanctify 140

Scoliosis 124

Sequence 148

Settle 60

Signatory 64

Silicone 84

Skull 28

Smallpox 88

Spacious 116

Specific 124

Specious 116

Systemic 112

T

Telekinesis 52

Temerarious 52

Tenuous 104

Terrific 124

Thesis 52

Tractable 88

Transgress 20

Troglodyte 56

Tuberculosis 124

Tycoon 20

U

Unsettle 60

V

Verbose 44

Viable 88

Vicarious 52

Vilify 40

Vociferous 104

W

Worldview 140

ACKNOWLEDGMENTS

The author would like to thank his colleagues and students for their invaluable assistance in bringing this book to life.

The author and publisher are grateful to those who have made this publication possible by providing all kinds of support from editing, graphic design, and proof-reading. Efforts have been made to identify the source of materials used in this book, however, it has not always been possible to identify the sources of all the materials used, or to trace the copyright holders. If any omissions are brought to our attention, we will be happy to include the appropriate acknowledgments on reprinting.

ABOUT THE AUTHOR

Dr. Richard Lee is a professor of English and distinguished publishing scholar with numerous books published under his name. His books are available on Amazon, other online stores, and in bookstores worldwide. He pursued his doctoral education at the University of Rochester in New York and the University of British Columbia and received his Ph.D. in English.

Printed in Great Britain
by Amazon.co.uk, Ltd.,
Marston Gate.